COOKING F(

Christmas

Choosing the menu is part of the excitement in the lead-up to the festive season. Will it be the traditional roast turkey, goose or rib of beef, or perhaps you favour Duck à L'Orange or Turkey Salad with Cranberry Vinaigrette? Whatever your preference, you're sure to find it here. Packed with family favourites and new ideas to try, this festive collection contains everything you need to celebrate the season with stylish food prepared and served with the minimum of fuss. On offer are fabulous finger foods for that perfect drinks and nibbles party, plus tried and true – and interesting new – food combinations for Christmas Day's special brunch, lunch or dinner. You'll have fun in the kitchen and enjoy the pleasure of giving more than ever before with this season's best dainty savouries, cakes and cookies, and gourmet gift ideas. Merry Christmas!

CONTENTS

FANCY FINGER FOOD

Whether you're catering for 6 or 60, get your celebration off to a great start with this delicious selection of savoury nibbles and finger food. Simple yet elegant, many of this chapter's ideas can be prepared in advance.

Mortadella Wedges

These pretty pink, white and green wedges are delicious with drinks.

6 slices mortadella sausage

Cheese Filling

250g (8oz) cream cheese, softened

3 tblspn finely chopped fresh parsley

2 tblspn snipped fresh chives

2 tblspn double cream

squeeze of lemon juice

pinch cayenne pepper or dash Tabasco sauce

1 To make filling, beat cream cheese until light. Beat in parsley, chives, cream, lemon juice and cayenne pepper or Tabasco to taste. Spread 5 mortadella slices thinly with cheese mixture and layer in a neat stack. Top with remaining mortadella slice.

2 Wrap stack in plastic food wrap and refrigerate until required. To serve, cut into 12 wedges and arrange on a serving plate.

Makes 12

Cheese Wafers

Keep a batch of unbaked dough in the freezer and slice or shape and bake as needed.

125g (4oz) finely grated mature Cheddar cheese, at room temperature

185g (6oz) butter, softened

185g (6oz) plain flour

1 tspn paprika

1 tspn salt

1/4 tspn freshly ground black pepper

2 tblspn toasted sesame seeds

1 Beat cheese and butter until creamy. Sift together flour, paprika, salt and black pepper and stir into creamed mixture with sesame seeds.

2 Shape dough into a 4cm (1¹/₂in) thick log. Wrap in plastic food wrap or foil and refrigerate for 1 hour.

3 Preheat oven to 180°C (350°F/ Gas 4). Cut log into thin slices and place on ungreased baking sheets. Bake for 10-12 minutes or until golden. Cool completely. Store in airtight containers.

Makes 30

Variations
Cheese Daisies: Press partially chilled dough through a biscuit press fitted with a flower nozzle onto baking sheets. Roll little balls of dough in poppy seeds and push into centres of flowers. Bake for 12-15 minutes.
Sesame Cheese Straws: Roll out chilled dough to 3-5mm (¹/₈-¹/₄in) thick and cut into 8cm x 5mm (3¹/₄ x ¹/₄in) straws. Bake for 10-12 minutes.
Cheese Almond Shortbreads: Omit paprika. Substitute 60g (2oz) of the flour with 90g (3oz) ground rice. Substitute sesame seeds with 2 tablespoons finely chopped almonds and add a pinch cayenne pepper. Shape dough into a log, chill, then cut into 3mm (¹/₈in) thick slices. Brush biscuits lightly with cold water and sprinkle with extra almonds. Bake for 12-15 minutes.

Mushroom Turnovers

60g (2oz) butter

4 spring onions, chopped

250g (8oz) mushrooms, finely chopped

1 tblspn lemon juice

60g (2oz) ham, chopped

60g (2oz) sour cream

freshly ground black pepper

beaten egg, for glaze

sesame seeds

Cream Cheese Pastry

125g (4oz) cream cheese, softened

125g (4oz) butter, softened

185g (6oz) plain flour, sifted

1 To make pastry, beat cream cheese and butter until creamy. Stir in flour to make a soft dough. Wrap and chill for several hours or overnight. (If left overnight, allow dough to stand at room temperature for 1 hour before rolling; it is soft and light so handle with care).

2 Melt butter in a frying pan over moderate heat and cook onions until soft. Add mushrooms and lemon juice and cook, stirring, for 5 minutes. Remove from heat and stir in ham, sour cream and black pepper to taste. Cool.

3 Preheat oven to 200°C (400°F/ Gas 6). Roll out pastry thinly and cut into 6cm (2¹/₂in) rounds with a fluted cutter, or the rim of a glass, dipped into flour between each cut. Place a teaspoonful of mushroom mixture on each round, moisten edges with beaten egg, fold over to form a turnover and seal edges with a fork. Brush with egg and sprinkle with sesame seeds. Place on ungreased baking sheets and bake for 10 minutes or until golden.

Makes 36

Kitchen Tip
Turnovers can be prepared for baking a day in advance and refrigerated, covered, on baking sheets. Bake as directed just before serving.

Mortadella Wedges, Cheese Wafers, Mushroom Turnovers, Cheese Daisies; Baba Ganouj (page 4)

Baba Ganouj

Use this recipe and your microwave to make a speedy version of this popular Middle Eastern dish.

2 medium aubergines

3 cloves garlic, crushed

3 tblspn olive oil

2 tblspn lemon juice

freshly ground black pepper

2-3 tblspn chopped fresh parsley

toasted pitta bread and olives to serve

1 Pierce aubergines several times with a fork and cook on HIGH (100%) for 4-6 minutes or until soft. Set aside. Combine garlic and 1 tablespoon olive oil in a small dish, cover and cook for 1-2 minutes.

2 Halve aubergines and scrape flesh into a bowl. Add lemon juice and mash with a fork to make a coarse purée.

3 Add garlic mixture to purée and gradually beat in remaining oil to make a thick paste. Season to taste with black pepper, then stir in parsley. Cover with plastic food wrap until required. Serve warm or at room temperature with pitta bread and olives as a first course or salad.

Serves 6

Onion Cumin Tart

This tart is best served soon after baking.

300g (9¹/₂oz) prepared puff pastry

1 egg white

45g (1¹/₂oz) butter

1 tspn cumin seeds

2 large onions, finely sliced

2 eggs

170ml (5¹/₂fl oz) double cream

freshly ground black pepper

1 Roll out pastry to line a 23cm (9in) flan tin with removable base. Cover pastry with baking paper, fill with dried beans and chill for 30 minutes.

2 Preheat oven to 200°C (400°F/ Gas 6). Bake pastry for 20 minutes or until just firm. Remove beans and paper, brush with egg white and cook for 3-5 minutes longer or until golden. Cool.

3 Melt butter in a frying pan over moderate heat until hot and foaming, add cumin seeds and onions and cook, stirring, until onions are soft and transparent. Drain well. Whisk together eggs, cream and black pepper to taste.

4 Reduce oven to 180°C (350°F/ Gas 4). Spread onions evenly in pastry case. Pour in egg mixture and bake for 15-20 minutes or until golden. Serve warm cut into wedges.

Serves 8-10

Savoury Pastry Puffs

Puffs can be filled and glazed a day in advance. Cover and chill until ready to bake.

500g (1lb) prepared puff pastry

2 eggs beaten with 2 tspn double cream

Olive Filling

155g (5oz) bottled olive paste

Blue Cheese Filling

185g (6oz) blue vein cheese (Roquefort, Stilton, Danish blue), crumbled

a little double cream

1 To make olive puffs, roll out half the pastry on a lightly floured surface to make a 30 x 25cm (12 x 10in) rectangle and cut in half lengthwise. Spread one half with olive paste. Top with uncovered half and press gently with rolling pin. Cut in half lengthwise, then cut crosswise into 6 x 3cm (2¹/₂ x 1¹/₄in) fingers.

2 Preheat oven to 200°C (400°F/ Gas 6). Place olive puffs on a baking sheet and brush with beaten egg mixture. Bake for 15-20 minutes or until golden. Serve hot.

3 To make cheese puffs, preheat oven to 220°C (425°F/Gas 7). Roll out remaining pastry thinly, cut into 6cm (2¹/₂in) rounds, place on baking sheets and brush with egg mixture. Bake for 8-10 minutes or until puffed and golden. Cool slightly.

4 Mash cheese with enough cream to make a smooth paste. Split pastries and pipe or spoon filling onto bottom halves. Top with remaining pastry halves and serve.

Makes 40 olive puffs and 28-30 cheese puffs

Kitchen Tip
Olive paste is available at speciality food shops. It can be made by stoning and puréeing the flesh of black olives with a little olive oil to make a smooth paste.

Chicory with Herb Cheese

250g (8oz) cream cheese, softened

4 tblspn snipped fresh chives

4 tblspn finely chopped walnuts

1 tblspn paprika

2 tblspn grated onion

2 tblspn sour cream

1 tspn Dijon mustard

4 heads of chicory

finely chopped walnuts, extra, for garnish

Combine all ingredients, except chicory and walnuts for garnish, and mix well. Cut off base of chicory, break off leaves and spread about 1 teaspoon cheese mixture on base of each leaf. Sprinkle cheese mixture with extra walnuts. Cover with plastic food wrap and chill until ready to serve.

Makes about 40

From the Top: Beef Fillet with Horseradish Cream, Chicory with Herb Cheese, Onion Cumin Tart, Savoury Pastry Puffs

Beef Fillet with Horseradish Cream

Roast fillet and prepare the cream the day before, wrap well and chill. Bring beef to room temperature to serve. Horseradish Cream is also delicious with smoked salmon on open faced sandwiches and canapés.

1 whole beef fillet, at room temperature, trimmed and tied to hold its shape

3 tblspn crushed black peppercorns

3 tblspn olive oil

1 French breadstick, sliced

watercress sprigs or lettuce leaves, for garnish

Horseradish Cream

2 tspn gelatine

60ml (2fl oz) water

250g (8oz) sour cream

2 tblspn bottled horseradish

2 tblspn chopped fresh parsley

1 Preheat oven to 250°C (500°F/ Gas 9). Pat fillet dry and coat well on all sides with black pepper. In a roasting tin just large enough to hold beef, heat oil over high heat until hot but not smoking. Add beef and brown on all sides. Place tin in oven and roast beef for 15-17 minutes for medium rare. Cool to room temperature.

2 To make Horseradish Cream, soften gelatine in cold water, then stir over hot water until dissolved. Stir together sour cream, horseradish and parsley, add gelatine and mix well. Spoon into a bowl, cover and chill until set.

3 To serve, slice beef into 1cm (1/2in) thick slices, arrange on sliced bread with a little watercress or lettuce and a spoonful of chilled Horseradish Cream. Serve garnished with watercress sprigs.

Serves 20-25

Kitchen Tip
Depending on the size of the fillet you may need to cut it in half before cooking.

Egg Mousse with Caviar

12 hard-boiled eggs

125g (4oz) sour cream

1 tblspn gelatine dissolved in 60ml (2fl oz) water

125g (4oz) thick mayonnaise

3 tblspn snipped fresh chives

2 tblspn lemon juice

1 tblspn Worcestershire sauce

1 tspn salt

1 tspn dry mustard mixed with a little water to make a paste

1/4 tspn ground white pepper

Tabasco sauce

black or red lumpfish roe for garnish

pumpernickel bread to serve

1 Chop eggs, then force through a coarse sieve into a bowl. Fold in sour cream and gelatine mixture. Add mayonnaise, chives, lemon juice, Worcestershire sauce, salt, mustard paste, white pepper and Tabasco sauce to taste and mix well. Spoon into a lightly oiled 20cm (8in) round cake tin, smoothing the top. Cover and chill for at least 4 hours.

2 Run a knife around edge of mousse to loosen, dip mould briefly into hot water and invert onto a serving plate, giving the mould a sharp rap to loosen the mousse. Decorate with red or black roe and serve with bread.

Serves 8

Kitchen Tip
This is easy to turn out if you use a small springform tin, or if you prefer, you can just shape it into a round on a serving plate.

Cheese Tartlets

250g (8oz) plain flour

1/2 tspn salt

125g (4oz) butter, chilled and diced

3 tblspn iced water

Cheddar and Olive Filling

1 1/2 tblspn chopped black olives

2 1/2 tblspn milk

freshly ground black pepper

125g (4oz) grated mature Cheddar cheese

1 egg, beaten

Stilton Filling

90g (3oz) Stilton or other blue cheese, crumbled

4 tblspn double cream

1 egg, beaten

2 tspn cherry-flavoured liqueur, optional

freshly ground black pepper

1 Sift flour and salt into a bowl. Rub in butter until mixture resembles coarse breadcrumbs. Gradually add water, mixing to make a smooth dough. Shape into a ball, wrap and chill for 30 minutes.

2 Roll out pastry and using a 7.5cm (3in) cutter, cut out 20 rounds. Place rounds in tartlet tins and chill for 15 minutes. Preheat oven to 200°C (400°F/Gas 6).

3 To make Cheddar and Olive Filling, combine olives, milk and black pepper to taste in a saucepan, bring to the boil, reduce heat and simmer for 5 minutes. Remove from heat, stir in Cheddar cheese and egg and cool. Spoon mixture into half the tartlet cases.

4 To make Stilton filling, combine Stilton cheese, cream, egg, liqueur (if using) and black pepper to taste and spoon into remaining tartlet cases. Bake tartlets for 15 minutes or until golden. Serve warm.

Makes 20 tartlets

Rosemary Biscuits

125g (4oz) butter

125g (4oz) cream cheese, softened

125g (4oz) plain flour, sifted

1 tspn finely chopped fresh rosemary

pinch cayenne pepper, optional

1 Beat together butter and cream cheese until well blended. Add flour, rosemary and cayenne (if using) and mix with a fork until combined.

2 Shape dough into two rolls, each 4cm (1 1/2in) in diameter. Wrap separately and chill for several hours or overnight (pastry can be frozen indefinitely).

3 Preheat oven to 220°C (425°F/Gas 7). Cut rolls into 5mm (1/4in) thick slices, place on greased baking sheets and bake for 8-10 minutes or until golden.

Makes about 60

Smoked Fish Pâté

The microwave makes short work of this pâté.

250g (8oz) kippers or smoked mackerel

1 small onion, chopped

60g (2oz) butter

90g (3oz) cream cheese, softened

1/4 tspn grated nutmeg

1 tblspn lemon juice

freshly ground black pepper

fresh parsley sprigs for garnish

toast triangles or cracker biscuits to serve

1 Place fish in a shallow microwavable dish, cover and cook on HIGH (100%) for 4 minutes, turning once. Set aside. Place onion and butter in a microwavable bowl, cover and cook for 2 minutes.

2 Remove skin and bones from fish and chop roughly. Place in a blender or food processor with onion mixture, cream cheese, nutmeg, lemon juice and black pepper to taste and process until smooth.

3 Place mixture in a serving dish or divide between four small ramekins, cool completely, cover and chill for 2 hours. Garnish with parsley and serve as a first course or with drinks with toast or crackers.

Serves 4 as a first course

Egg Mousse with Caviar, Shortbread (page 18), Cheese Tartlets,
Cheese Almond Shortbreads (page 2), Rosemary Biscuits

Rumaki

Rumaki can be made well ahead, stored with marinade in a covered container in the refrigerator and grilled as required.

1-2 tblspn groundnut (peanut) oil

500g (1lb) chicken livers, cleaned and trimmed

2 tspn grated fresh ginger

1 clove garlic, crushed

125ml (4fl oz) soy sauce

2 tblspn rice wine or dry sherry

2 tspn sesame oil

220g (7oz) canned whole water chestnuts, drained

250g (8oz) bacon rashers, rind removed

1 Heat groundnut (peanut) oil in a frying pan over high heat and sauté livers for 2-3 minutes or until light brown. Combine ginger, garlic, soy sauce, wine or sherry and sesame oil in a bowl, add livers and marinate for at least 30 minutes, longer if possible.

2 Cut water chestnuts into thick slices. Cut each bacon rasher into three pieces. Drain livers, wrap each with a slice of chestnut in a piece of bacon and secure with a toothpick.

3 Cook under a preheated medium grill, turning several times, for 5-8 minutes or until bacon is golden and livers cooked. Serve warm.

Makes 36-40

Parmesan Sticks

250g (8oz) prepared puff pastry

freshly grated Parmesan cheese

1 egg white, lightly beaten

paprika

1 Preheat oven to 200°C (400°F/ Gas 6). Roll out pastry on a lightly floured surface to a make a 30 x 25cm (12 x 10in) rectangle. Sprinkle generously with cheese and gently roll to press cheese into pastry.

2 Prick pastry all over with a fork, brush with egg white and sprinkle lightly with more cheese and paprika. Lightly roll again to press cheese into pastry. Cut in half lengthwise, then crosswise into 2cm (3/4in) wide strips.

3 Place strips on dampened baking sheets, twisting them if desired. Bake for 10 minutes or until crisp and golden. Cool completely and store in an airtight container. Place in a hot oven to crispen for a few minutes before serving.

Makes 30

Liptauer

250g (8oz) butter, softened

1 tblspn caraway seeds, crushed

1 tblspn dry mustard

1 tblspn snipped fresh chives

1 tblspn capers, finely chopped

1 canned anchovy fillet, finely chopped

250g (8oz) cottage or ricotta cheese, sieved

1 tblspn paprika

radishes and celery sticks for garnish

assorted cracker biscuits to serve

1 Beat butter until creamy then beat in caraway seeds, mustard, chives, capers and anchovy until combined. Gradually beat in cottage or ricotta cheese until blended.

2 Spoon mixture into a bowl or shape into a mound on a small platter. Sprinkle with paprika, garnish with radishes and celery and serve with crackers.

Makes 500g (1lb)

Crab and Almond Mushrooms

25-30 small mushroom caps, stems removed

homemade or bottled vinaigrette dressing

220g (7oz) fresh or canned flaked crab meat or cooked chopped chicken

2 tblspn chopped fresh parsley

2 tblspn chopped spring onions

2 tblspn mayonnaise

60g (2oz) chopped toasted almonds

lemon juice

freshly ground black pepper

1 Wipe mushrooms with a damp cloth and brush insides with a little dressing.

2 Combine crab meat or chicken, parsley, spring onions, mayonnaise, almonds, lemon juice and black pepper to taste. Fill mushrooms with mixture. Cover and chill until ready to serve.

Makes 25-30

Liver and Sage Crostini

2 tblspn unsalted butter

2 tblspn chopped onion

1 tblspn capers, chopped

6 fresh sage leaves or 1/2 tspn dried sage

2 tblspn dry sherry

freshly ground black pepper

2 tblspn olive oil

500g (1lb) chicken livers, trimmed and chopped

thick slices of French bread

1/2 bunch fresh parsley, chopped

125g (4oz) freshly grated Parmesan cheese

1 lemon, cut in wedges

1 Melt butter in a frying pan over moderately low heat and cook onion until soft. Add capers, sage, sherry and black pepper to taste and simmer, stirring, until most of the liquid evaporates. Transfer to a blender or food processor.

2 In clean pan, heat 1 tablespoon oil over moderately high heat and sauté livers for 1-2 minutes or until brown on the outside but still pink inside. Add to onion mixture and process to make a coarse purée.

3 Brush bread slices with remaining oil and toast under a preheated low grill for 3-4 minutes or until crisp. Mound liver mixture in a bowl, mix parsley and Parmesan cheese in another bowl, place toast into a bread basket and lemon wedges in a dish. The idea is to spread pâté on the toast, add a squeeze of lemon, and a topping of cheese.

Makes 500g (1lb)

Prawns with Mango Sauce

50 cooked medium prawns

50 sugar snap peas or mangetout

50 toothpicks

Mango Sauce

1 fresh mango or 1/2 of 440g (14oz) canned sliced mango, drained

125ml (4fl oz) olive oil

6-10 fresh mint leaves

2 tblspn lemon juice

freshly ground black pepper

1 Peel and devein prawns and refrigerate. Trim peas or mangetout and plunge into boiling water. Remove immediately and refresh under cold running water. Wrap a prawn around each pea and secure with a toothpick. Place on a platter, cover and refrigerate until required.

2 To make sauce, peel mango, scrape flesh into a blender or food processor and purée. Add oil, mint leaves, lemon juice and black pepper to taste and process until combined. Serve at room temperature with prawns.

Makes 50

Quail Egg Tartlets

If quail eggs are not available, use a slice of hard-boiled hens egg for each tart.

25 quail eggs

125g (4oz) Homemade Mayonnaise (page 26)

60g (2oz) pesto, purchased or homemade (page 26)

25 homemade or purchased tiny pastry cases

1 Cook eggs in gently simmering water for 3-4 minutes. Drain and refresh under cold running water, peel and place in a bowl. Cover with cold water and refrigerate up to 2 days, if needed, before using.

2 Several hours before serving, combine mayonnaise and pesto. Smear a little pesto mayonnaise in base of each tartlet. Slice a sliver off each egg and place, cut-side-down, in tartlets. Spoon more pesto mayonnaise over eggs. Cover and chill until ready to serve.

Makes 25

Liptauer, Crab and Almond Mushrooms, Liver and Sage Crostini, Parmesan Sticks (page 7)

Baby Brioche Sandwiches

Use the smallest brioche tins available or tiny patty tins for this recipe. Keep the dough, covered, in the refrigerator while each batch of brioche bakes. You can vary the fillings if desired; try prosciutto and goat's cheese, salmon and cucumber, eggs and asparagus, chicken and walnuts or roast beef and watercress.

500g (1lb) cream cheese, softened

3-4 tblspn finely chopped fresh herbs, such as dill, chives, parsley

2-3 tblspn grated onion

Tabasco sauce or lemon juice

125g (4oz) sliced pastrami or smoked salmon, cut into 3-4 pieces

Brioche Dough

10g (1/3oz) fresh yeast or 1 tspn dried yeast

2 tblspn warm water

250g (8oz) plain flour

1 1/2 tblspn caster sugar

1/2 tspn salt

3 eggs

155g (5oz) unsalted butter, melted and cooled

1 egg yolk mixed with 1 tspn water and pinch salt

1 To make dough, mix yeast and warm water to a paste. Fit food processor with plastic blade, add flour, sugar and salt and process briefly to combine.

2 Add eggs, butter and yeast mixture to flour and process until just combined. Transfer to a buttered bowl, press a piece of plastic food wrap onto surface of dough and cover bowl tightly with more wrap. Refrigerate overnight.

3 Break off small pieces of dough, roll into balls and place in 35-38 tiny brioche tins, filling them no more than half-full. For top knots, break off hazelnut-size pieces of dough, roll into balls and shape one end into a point. With a floured finger, make a hole in centre of brioches and place the pointed end of each knot into holes.

4 Place tins on a baking sheet, cover with a tea-towel and set aside in a warm place until dough rises to two-thirds fill tins.

5 Preheat oven to 200°C (400°F/Gas 6). Brush tops of brioches with egg yolk mixture and bake for 15-18 minutes or until golden. Stand 5 minutes in tins before turning out to cool.

6 Beat cream cheese until smooth, then stir in herbs, onion and Tabasco sauce or lemon juice to taste. Slice brioches in half, liberally spread both halves with cheese mixture, then sandwich together with a piece of pastrami or salmon. Cover and store in a cool place for no longer than 3-4 hours before serving.

Makes 35-38

Kitchen Tip

Prepare the brioche well ahead of the day and store in the freezer. Simply refresh and fill several hours before guests arrive. If you're planning to freeze your brioche, place in freezer bags and seal well. When ready to use, do not thaw, but place on a baking sheet and bake from frozen at 180°C (350°F/Gas 4) for about 5 minutes or until heated.

Asparagus Prosciutto Fingers

Green beans, thin wedges of cantaloupe or thin, crisp Italian breadsticks can be used in place of the asparagus if you wish.

50 spears fresh asparagus

25 thin slices prosciutto or ham

1 Trim asparagus spears. Drop into a large saucepan of boiling water; allow water to return to the boil, then remove immediately and refresh under cold running water. Drain well.

2 Cut prosciutto slices in half lengthwise, wind half a slice around each asparagus spear and arrange on a platter. Cover and keep cool until ready to serve.

Makes 50

Smoked Salmon and Roe Toasts

19-25 slices white sandwich bread

315g (10oz) sour cream

100g (3 1/2oz) thinly sliced smoked salmon, finely chopped

100g (3 1/2oz) salmon roe or black or red lumpfish roe

1 Preheat oven to 180°C (350°F/ Gas 4). Using a small fancy cutter, cut out 50 shapes from the bread. Place shapes on a baking sheet and bake for 10-12 minutes or until dried out and lightly coloured. Cool completely and store in an airtight container.

2 Just prior to serving, place 1 teaspoon sour cream and 1/2 teaspoon each of salmon and roe on each toast shape, then arrange attractively on a serving platter.

Makes 50

Chicory with Herb Cheese (page 4), Baby Brioche Sandwiches, Asparagus Prosciutto Fingers, Quail Egg Tartlets (page 8), Smoked Salmon and Roe Toasts, Prawns with Mango Sauce (page 8)

CHRISTMAS BAKING & GOURMET GIFTS

Treat special friends with these fabulous gourmet gift ideas. There are cookies and festive cakes to bake, a homemade mincemeat with which to create fabulous Christmas pies and tarts and preserves to make any meal a special occasion.

Bishop's Cake

A little of this goes a long way so slice very thinly. The cake takes its name from the stained-glass window effect of the colourful slices.

500g (1lb) Brazil nuts

12 pitted dates

2 glacé pineapple rings, cut into chunks

6 glacé apricots

185g (6oz) mixed red and green glacé cherries

90g (3oz) plain flour

1/2 tspn baking powder

1/2 tspn salt

3 eggs

170g (5 1/2 oz) caster sugar

1 tspn vanilla essence

1 Preheat oven to 150°C (300°F/ Gas 4). Grease a 21 x 11cm (8 1/2 x 4 1/2 in) loaf tin and line base and sides with greaseproof paper. Alternatively, grease a ring tin and line with well greased foil.

2 Place nuts, dates, pineapple, apricots and cherries in a bowl. Sift flour, baking powder and salt over top of fruit. Beat eggs until frothy, add sugar and beat until thick. Stir in vanilla essence. Pour over fruit mixture and mix well.

3 Spoon mixture into prepared tin and bake for 1 3/4 hours for loaf or 1 1/4 - 1 1/2 hours for ring or until cooked when tested with a skewer. Turn cake onto a wire rack, remove from tin and allow to cool. Wrap cake in foil and store in the refrigerator.

Makes 1 cake

Christmas Mince Pies

1 quantity Christmas Mincemeat (page 15)

1 beaten egg and extra caster sugar to glaze

Rich Shortcrust Pastry

315g (10oz) plain flour

1/2 tspn salt

185g (6oz) butter, cut into pieces

1 tblspn caster sugar

1 egg yolk blended with 2 tblspn iced water

1 To make pastry, sift flour and salt into a bowl. Rub in butter with fingertips until mixture resembles breadcrumbs. Stir in 1 tablespoon sugar and make a well in the centre. Add egg yolk mixture and mix to make a dough. Knead lightly on a floured surface until smooth. Wrap and chill for 1 hour.

2 Preheat oven to 190°C (375°F/ Gas 5). Roll half the pastry thinly into a rectangle. Cut out twelve rounds to fit small greased tartlet or patty tins. Cut out twelve more rounds for lids of pies.

3 Fill pastry cases with mincemeat and cover with pastry lids. Decorate lids with cut-outs of stars or slits, if liked, and press edges to seal. Brush with beaten egg and sprinkle with extra sugar.

4 Bake for 25 minutes or until golden. Stand briefly in tins before turning out. Serve warm or cold.

Makes 12

Bishop's Cake, Christmas Mince Pies

Traditional Christmas Cake

Bake well ahead so it can mature, but do not ice more than a week before Christmas.

375g (12oz) raisins, chopped

250g (8oz) sultanas

125g (4oz) currants

125g (4oz) glacé cherries, cut in half

3 tblspn sherry

4 tblspn brandy

125g (4oz) dried apricots, chopped

2 tblspn hot water

250g (8oz) butter

220g (7oz) soft brown sugar

2 tspn finely grated lemon rind

1 tblspn golden syrup

2 tblspn marmalade

5 eggs

315g (10oz) plain flour

1 tspn mixed spice

1 tspn cinnamon

1/4 tspn salt

125g (4oz) blanched almonds, chopped

extra almonds to decorate, if cake is not to be iced

1 The day before baking, mix raisins, sultanas, currants, cherries, sherry and 3 tablespoons brandy in a bowl. Soak apricots in hot water for 1 hour, then add to fruit mixture. Cover and macerate overnight.

2 Grease and line a deep 23cm (9in) square cake tin. Preheat oven to 150°C (300°F/Gas 2).

3 Beat butter, brown sugar and lemon rind until fluffy. Beat in golden syrup and marmalade. Add eggs, one at a time, beating well after each addition. If mixture curdles, stir in a tablespoon of the flour with each egg.

4 Sift together flour, spices and salt and fold into egg mixture, alternately, with fruit mixture and chopped almonds. Turn into prepared tin. Decorate top with whole almonds if you do not intend to ice the cake.

5 Bake on centre shelf of oven for 4 hours or until cooked when tested with a skewer. Remove from the oven and sprinkle with 1 tablespoon brandy. Cool cake in tin. Store wrapped in a tea-towel in an airtight container.

Makes 1 cake

To Ice the Christmas Cake

Allow 3 days for covering and icing the cake.

Glaze

2 tblspn sieved apricot jam

1 1/2 tblspn water

1/4 tspn lemon juice

Almond Paste

185g (6oz) ground almonds

90g (3oz) caster sugar

90g (3oz) icing sugar

1 tspn lemon juice

1 egg yolk

2-3 drops almond essence

Royal Icing

2 egg whites

500g (1lb) pure icing sugar, sifted

1 tspn lemon juice

1 Just prior to covering the cake with Almond Paste brush with warm glaze. To make glaze, place jam and water in a saucepan and simmer for 4 minutes, add lemon juice and simmer until glaze coats a wooden spoon.

2 To make Almond Paste, sift together almonds and sugars. Add lemon juice, egg yolk and almond essence, mix well and knead lightly. Roll out to fit the top of the cake, place in position, trim edges and smooth the surface. Leave for 48 hours. If paste seems sticky, roll out on a surface sprinkled with sifted icing sugar.

3 To make icing, beat egg whites until frothy then gradually beat in icing sugar. Add lemon juice and beat to soft peaks. Spread over cake and rough the surface to resemble snow. Add decorations and allow to set before cutting.

Kitchen Tip

To prepare a cake tin for baking a dense fruit cake, grease the tin, then line the base and sides with a layer of greased brown paper, then a double thickness of greased, greaseproof or baking paper, trimming neatly to fit into corners.

Boiled Whisky Fruit Cake

750g (1 1/2lb) mixed dried fruit

185g (6oz) butter

185ml (6fl oz) water

220g (7oz) brown sugar

60ml (2fl oz) whisky

3 large eggs

125g (4oz) plain flour

185g (6oz) self-raising flour

1 1/2 tspn mixed spice

1/2 tspn bicarbonate of soda

1/4 tspn salt

1 Grease and line a deep 20cm (8in) cake tin. Preheat oven to 180°C (350°F/Gas 4).

2 Place fruit in a saucepan, add butter, water and brown sugar and slowly bring to the boil. Reduce heat and simmer for 5 minutes. Remove from heat and set aside to cool until lukewarm.

3 Add whisky, then beat in eggs, one at a time. Sift together flours, spice, bicarbonate of soda and salt, add to mixture and mix well to combine.

4 Spoon into prepared tin and bake for 45 minutes. Reduce oven temperature to 160°C (325°F/Gas 3) and bake for 45 minutes longer or until a skewer inserted into centre comes out clean.

5 Stand cake briefly in tin, then turn onto a wire rack to cool. Remove paper when cold.

Makes 1 cake

Apple Mincemeat Tart, Ginger Rum Ice Cream (page 42)

Apple Mincemeat Tart

1 quantity Rich Shortcrust Pastry from Christmas Mince Pies (page 12)

625g (1¹/₄lb) Christmas Mincemeat, recipe follows

220g (7oz) grated Granny Smith apples

1 egg white to glaze

sugar to glaze

1 Prepare and chill pastry following recipe directions. Roll out three-quarters of the dough on a lightly floured surface to line a 23cm (9in) pie plate. Trim edges. Combine mincemeat and apples, spoon into pastry case and chill.

2 Roll out remaining pastry and cut into 1cm (¹/₂in) wide strips. Weave strips into a lattice on a piece of baking paper and chill until firm. Gently slide lattice off paper onto filling, pressing edges to pastry case, and trim.

3 Preheat oven to 190°C (375°F/ Gas 5). Beat egg white until foamy, brush over lattice, then sprinkle with sugar. Bake tart for 45 minutes or until pastry is golden. Serve warm with whipped cream or vanilla ice cream.

Serves 6-8

Christmas Mincemeat

250g (8oz) shredded suet

60g (2oz) blanched almonds, finely chopped

125g (4oz) candied peel, finely chopped

1 Granny Smith apple, peeled and chopped

60g (2oz) glacé cherries, chopped

60g (2oz) glacé ginger, chopped

750g (1¹/₂lb) mixed dried fruit

250g (8oz) soft brown sugar

¹/₄ tspn salt

¹/₄ tspn ground nutmeg

¹/₄ tspn ground mixed spice

grated rind and juice of 1 orange

grated rind and juice of 1 lemon

125ml (4fl oz) brandy or rum

1 Remove any fibres from suet and mix with almonds, peel and apple. Add cherries, ginger and mixed fruit and mix to combine.

2 Set aside one-third of mixture and coarsely mince the rest. Combine fruit mixtures. Stir in sugar, salt, spices, citrus rinds and juices and brandy or rum.

3 Pack mincemeat into sterilised jars, cover with circles of greaseproof paper dipped in brandy, then cover with lids to seal.

Makes about 1.25kg (2¹/₂lb)

Kitchen Tip
Beef suet is added to mincemeat to help preserve it. When heated, the suet melts, giving a wonderful richness. You can buy it at some grocers or prepare your own from good suet bought from the butcher. The food processor is excellent for shredding suet, especially if you add 30g (1oz) plain flour before processing.

Rich Christmas Cake

750g (1¹/₂lb) raisins, chopped

375g (12oz) sultanas, chopped

250g (8oz) currants

125g (4oz) chopped mixed peel

4 dried pears, chopped

4 dried nectarines or peaches, chopped

125g (4oz) blanched almonds, chopped

2 tblspn brandy

2 tblspn rum

375g (12oz) plain flour

¹/₂ tspn baking powder

1 tspn mixed spice

250g (8oz) butter

220g (7oz) brown sugar

2 tspn finely grated lemon rind

5 eggs

90g (3oz) blanched whole almonds and
1 glacé cherry, optional

2-3 tblspn rum or brandy, extra

1 The day before baking, combine raisins, sultanas and currants in a large bowl. Add peel, pears, nectarines or peaches and almonds. Sprinkle with brandy and rum, cover and macerate at room temperature overnight.

2 Grease and line a deep 25cm (10in) cake tin. Preheat oven to 150°C (300°F/Gas 2). Sift together flour, baking powder and spice. Toss 2 tablespoons of flour mixture with fruit mixture.

3 Beat butter and sugar together until soft, add lemon rind and beat until fluffy. Add eggs, one at a time, beating well after each addition. Stir in remaining flour then fruit mixture.

4 Place mixture in prepared tin. Level top and drop tin sharply on kitchen bench to settle and remove air bubbles. Decorate with split whole almonds and place a cherry in the centre, if using.

5 Bake for 3¹/₂ hours or until cooked when tested. Turn cake upside down, lift paper, sprinkle hot cake with extra rum or brandy and reseal.

6 Wrap cake in a tea-towel and cool completely. Wrap in greaseproof paper, then in foil and store in a cool place until needed.

Makes 1 cake

Light Fruit Cake

250g (8oz) butter

220g (7oz) caster sugar

2-3 tspn finely grated orange rind

5 eggs

315g (10oz) plain flour

1 tspn baking powder

¹/₂ tspn salt

90g (3oz) blanched almonds, chopped

185g (6oz) sultanas

155g (5oz) currants

155g (5oz) raisins, halved

45g (1¹/₂oz) glacé cherries

30g (1oz) chopped mixed peel

2 tblspn fresh orange juice

extra almonds

1 Grease and line a deep 20cm (8in) round cake tin. Preheat oven to 150°C (300°F/Gas 2).

2 Beat butter, sugar and orange rind until creamy. Beat in eggs, one at a time, and set aside. In a separate bowl, sift together flour, baking powder and salt. Mix in almonds, dried fruits and peel.

3 Add dry mixture to creamed mixture, add orange juice and mix well to combine. Turn mixture into prepared tin, smooth the top and decorate with extra almonds.

4 Bake for 2¹/₂ hours or until a skewer inserted in centre comes out clean. Allow to cool in tin.

Makes 1 cake

Rich Christmas Cake, Light Fruit Cake; Cherry Almond Cake, Shortbread (page 18), Christmas Mince Pies (page 12); Apple Mincemeat Tart, Christmas Mincemeat (page 15)

Cherry Almond Cake

315g (10oz) butter	
280g (9oz) caster sugar	
2-3 drops almond essence	
5 eggs	
125g (4oz) glacé cherries	
60g (2oz) blanched almonds, chopped	
375g (12oz) plain flour	
1 tspn baking powder	
170ml (5¹/₂fl oz) milk	
6 glacé cherries and extra whole almonds to decorate	

1 Grease and line a deep 20cm (8in) cake tin with baking paper. Preheat oven to 180°C (350°F/Gas 4).

2 Beat butter, sugar and almond essence until light and fluffy. Add eggs, one at a time, beating well after each addition. Dust cherries and chopped almonds with a little of the flour. Sift remaining flour with baking powder and add to creamed mixture, alternately, with the milk. Fold in cherries and chopped almonds.

3 Place mixture in prepared tin and decorate top of cake with remaining cherries and whole almonds. Bake for 1¹/₂ hours or until cake is cooked when tested with a skewer. To prevent splitting and cracking on top, cover with 2-3 layers paper for the first 30 minutes of baking. Cool on a wire rack.

Makes 1 cake

Shortbread

250g (8oz) unsalted butter	
100g (3¹/₂oz) caster sugar	
500g (1lb) plain flour	

1 Preheat oven to 180°C (350°F/ Gas 4). Beat butter until it resembles whipped cream then gradually add sugar and continue beating until light and fluffy. Gradually mix in flour, then knead dough for 5 minutes or until very smooth.

2 Divide dough into three pieces, press into 20cm (8in) circles on baking sheets and crimp edge by pressing with fingers, or use a fork to decorate. Mark each circle into wedges.

3 Prick shortbread all over with a fork and bake on centre shelf of oven for 20 minutes. Reduce oven temperature to 150°C (300°F/Gas 2) and bake for 25 minutes longer or until golden and crisp. Cut through marks while shortbread is still warm then cool.

Makes 3 shortbreads

Sago Plum Pudding

This pudding mixture may be divided into six individual moulds and steamed for 1 hour, if preferred.

2 tblspn sago	
250ml (8fl oz) milk	
60g (2oz) butter	
250g (8oz) sugar	
1 tspn bicarbonate of soda	
pinch salt	
60g (2oz) breadcrumbs, made from stale bread	
155g (5oz) mixed dried fruit	
1 tblspn chopped mixed candied peel	
¹/₂ tspn mixed spice	

1 Soak sago in milk overnight. Beat butter and sugar until creamy then beat in undrained sago, bicarbonate of soda and salt. Add breadcrumbs, fruit, mixed peel and spice to mixture and mix well.

2 Place mixture in a well-greased pudding basin or mould. Cover top with greased greaseproof paper, then a double thickness of foil and tie securely.

3 Place basin on a rack in a large saucepan filled with enough boiling water to come halfway up sides of basin, cover pan and steam for 2 hours, adding more water as needed. Serve with custard or cream.

Serves 6

Christmas Pudding

250g (8oz) raisins	
60g (2oz) chopped mixed peel	
250g (8oz) sultanas	
125g (4oz) currants	
60g (2oz) blanched almonds, chopped	
3 tblspn rum or brandy	
250g (8oz) butter	
300g (9¹/₂oz) brown sugar	
2-3 tspn finely grated orange rind	
125g (4oz) plain flour	
1 tspn mixed spice	
¹/₂ tspn ground ginger	
4 eggs, beaten	
125g (4oz) breadcrumbs, made from stale bread	

1 Place all fruits and nuts in a large bowl, sprinkle with rum or brandy, cover and macerate overnight. Cream butter until soft, add sugar and orange rind and beat until light and fluffy.

2 Sift flour with spices, add to butter mixture, alternately, with eggs. Stir in breadcrumbs and fruit mixture and mix well. To wrap and cook the pudding, refer to Cooking the Christmas Pudding (see instructions following).

3 On Christmas Day, steam or boil again for 2¹/₂ hours. Turn pudding out onto a heated plate, warm 1-2 tablespoons rum or brandy, ignite and pour over pudding. Serve with custard or brandy butter.

Serves 8

Cooking the Christmas Pudding

To Steam: Place mixture into a well-greased china or aluminium pudding basin. Cover with greased foil. If the basin has a lid, place lid over foil and bring surplus foil up over it. If no lid is available, tie foil securely in position with string. Place basin on a rack or upturned saucer in a large saucepan with enough boiling water to come

Christmas Pudding

halfway up sides of basin, cover pan and steam for 6 hours, adding more boiling water as needed to maintain level. Remove from pan, cool completely and replace foil cover. Refrigerate pudding for up to six weeks. On the day, steam for 1 hour, turn out and serve.

To Tie and Boil: Dip pudding cloth into boiling water and wring out excess. Spread out on a flat surface, sprinkle centre with 5 tablespoons flour and rub into cloth, covering an area 38cm (15in) in diameter. Spoon pudding mixture onto centre, gather up four corners firmly around mixture and mould into a smooth, round shape. Tie cloth tightly as close to mixture as possible. Make a loop in string for easy lifting.

Three-quarters fill a large saucepan with water and bring to the boil. Quickly lower pudding into pan, cover and boil for 6 hours, adding more boiling water as needed to ensure pudding floats freely. Lift pudding from pan using a wooden spoon placed through the loop, drain and suspend from a drawer or cupboard handle so that it swings freely. Let dry overnight or until completely cold. Cut string, loosen cloth from top of pudding, remove excess flour and allow to dry completely — this could take a day or two. Retie cloth and store pudding in an airtight container in the refrigerator for up to 6 weeks. Remove pudding from refrigerator 12 hours before reheating. Boil again for 1 hour then suspend to drain for 10 minutes. Remove string, peel off cloth and allow to stand for 20 minutes before cutting.

Almond Brandy Butter

125g (4oz) unsalted butter

60g (2oz) icing sugar, sifted

60g (2oz) ground almonds

2-3 drops almond essence

1 tblspn orange-flavoured liqueur

1 tblspn brandy

1 egg white, stiffly beaten

Beat butter until light and fluffy and almost white. Gradually beat in icing sugar. Add almonds and enough almond essence to flavour. Beat in liqueur and brandy until creamy then fold in egg white. Mound mixture into a bowl, cover and store in the refrigerator.

Serves 8

Cranberry Chews

185g (6oz) plain flour, plus 2 tblspn extra

250g (8oz) brown sugar, plus 2 tblspn extra

125g (4oz) butter

250g (8oz) cranberry sauce

1 tblspn finely grated orange rind

2 eggs

1 tspn vanilla essence

60g (2oz) walnuts, roughly chopped

60g (2oz) shredded coconut

45g (1¹/₂oz) bran flake cereal with sultanas

1 Preheat oven to 180°C (350°F/ Gas 4). Place 185g (6oz) flour, 2 tablespoons sugar and butter in a food processor and process until mixture resembles breadcrumbs. Press mixture into a greased 30 x 22cm (12 x 8³/₄in) baking tin and bake for 10 minutes.

2 Combine cranberry sauce and orange rind and spread evenly over baked layer. Beat together eggs, remaining sugar, extra flour and vanilla essence until fluffy, stir in walnuts and coconut and spread over cranberry layer. Sprinkle with cereal.

3 Bake for 25 minutes or until topping is firm. Cool completely before cutting.

Makes 48

Snowballs

125g (4oz) crunchy peanut butter

2 tblspn softened butter

3 tblspn icing sugar, sifted

90g (3oz) sultanas, roughly chopped

45g (1¹/₂oz) sesame seeds, toasted

4 plain sweet biscuits, finely crushed

Stir together peanut butter and butter. Add sugar, sultanas and sesame seeds and mix well to combine. Shape mixture into 2cm (³/₄in) balls and roll in crushed biscuits. Cover and chill until firm.

Makes about 20

Cherry Almond Shortbread

125g (4oz) butter

60g (2oz) caster sugar

185g (6oz) plain flour, sifted

90g (3oz) slivered almonds

60g (2oz) glacé cherries, roughly chopped

Preheat oven to 180°C (350°F/ Gas 4). Beat butter and sugar until creamy. Add flour, almonds and cherries and mix well. Pack mixture into a well-greased 20cm (8in) square or round cake tin and mark into wedges or small squares. Bake for 20-25 minutes or until golden and crisp. Cut through marks while shortbread is still warm, then cool.

Makes 25

Coconut Choc Balls

90g (3oz) cream cheese, softened

1 tblspn water

1 tspn vanilla essence

315g (10oz) icing sugar, sifted

90g (3oz) dark chocolate, melted and slightly cooled

125g (4oz) pecans, chopped

desiccated coconut to coat

Beat together cream cheese, water and vanilla essence until creamy. Gradually add icing sugar, beating until blended. Stir in chocolate and nuts. Shape mixture into 2cm (³/₄in) balls and roll in coconut. Cover and chill until firm.

Makes 48

Cherry Almond Shortbread, Snowballs, Cranberry Chews, Coconut Choc Balls; Nut Crescents, Russian Tea Cakes (page 22)

Gingernuts

125g (4oz) plain flour

2 tblspn sugar

1 tspn bicarbonate of soda

1 tspn mixed spice

1 tspn ground cinnamon

1 tspn ground ginger

60g (2oz) butter

2 tblspn golden syrup

250g (8oz) sugar to coat, optional

1 Preheat oven to 240°C (475°F/ Gas 8). Sift together flour, 2 tablespoons sugar, bicarbonate of soda and spices. Melt butter with golden syrup, add to flour mixture and mix well.

2 Shape dough into walnut-size balls and if liked, roll in extra sugar for crunchiness. Place well apart on greased baking sheets and press down lightly. Bake for 5 minutes.

3 Reduce oven temperature to 180°C (350°/Gas 4) and bake for 7-10 minutes longer or until firm and golden. Loosen bisuits with a spatula and cool on baking sheets.

Makes 20

Pecan Cookies

155g (5oz) plain flour

1/2 tspn of salt

1/4 tspn bicarbonate of soda

125g (4oz) butter

45g (1 1/2oz) brown sugar

60g (2oz) caster sugar

1 egg, beaten

1 tspn vanilla essence

100g (3 1/2oz) chocolate chips

60g (2oz) pecans, chopped

36 pecan halves

1 Preheat oven to 180°C (350°F/ Gas 4). Sift together flour, salt and bicarbonate of soda. Beat butter with sugars until light and fluffy, add egg and vanilla essence and beat well until creamy. Stir flour mixture, chocolate chips and chopped pecans into egg mixture.

2 Drop teaspoons of mixture onto greased baking sheets, leaving room for spreading, and top each with a pecan half. Bake for 10 minutes or until firm and golden. Cool on wire racks.

Makes 36

Nut Crescents

250g (8oz) hazelnuts, ground

2 egg whites, unbeaten

220g (7oz) caster sugar

1 tspn vanilla essence

Preheat oven to 180°C (350°F/Gas 4). Place hazelnuts, egg whites, sugar and vanilla essence in a bowl and mix to combine. Shape mixture into small crescents and place on greased baking sheets. Bake for 15-18 minutes or until golden. Cool on wire racks.

Makes 30

Kitchen Tip

Grind nuts in a food processor or blender but take care not to overgrind or they will become oily. A few 'bits' add texture.

Russian Tea Cakes

250g (8oz) butter

100g (3 1/2oz) caster sugar

1 tspn vanilla essence

280g (9oz) plain flour

90g (3oz) ground pecans

extra caster sugar to coat

1 Beat together butter, sugar and vanilla essence until creamy. Add flour and pecans and mix to combine. Cover and chill until firm.

2 Preheat oven to 180°C (350°F/ Gas 4). Shape dough into 2cm (3/4in) balls and place on lightly greased baking sheets. Bake for 15-20 minutes or until firm and pale golden. While biscuits are still hot, roll in extra sugar, then cool on wire racks.

Makes 50

Coconut Buttons

125g (4oz) butter

220g (7oz) caster sugar

1 egg

250g (8oz) self-raising flour, sifted

pinch salt

90g (3oz) desiccated coconut

extra caster sugar to coat

glacé cherries, sliced, optional

1 Preheat oven to 190°C (375°F/ Gas 6). Beat butter and sugar until creamy then beat in egg. Stir in flour, salt and coconut.

2 Roll teaspoons of mixture into balls and press with the back of a spoon to flatten. Dip one side of each biscuit in extra sugar and place, sugar-side-up and well apart, on greased baking sheets. Top with cherry slices, if using.

3 Bake for 10-15 minutes or until golden. Loosen biscuits with a spatula, stand briefly on baking sheets then transfer to wire racks to cool.

Makes 40

Variation
To make Coconut Discs, follow recipe as directed but use only 125g (4oz) flour. This gives a thinner biscuit with a slightly chewy texture.

Christmas Butter Cookies

Christmas Butter Cookies

Use the picture as a guide and decorate dough as desired before baking. Or bake plain biscuits and decorate with icing after cooling.

375g (12oz) plain flour

2 tspn baking powder

pinch salt

250g (8oz) unsalted butter, cut into pieces

2 eggs

220g (7oz) caster sugar

1½ tspn vanilla essence

1 tspn finely grated lemon rind

1 egg white, lightly beaten to glaze

plain or coloured sugar to decorate

assorted cookie decorations

Cookie Icing, optional

155g (5oz) icing sugar

1 tblspn hot water

2-3 drops vanilla essence or lemon juice

food colouring, optional

1 Sift together flour, baking powder and salt. Rub in butter with fingertips until mixture resembles breadcrumbs. Make a well in centre of mixture.

2 Beat together eggs, sugar, vanilla essence and lemon rind, add to flour mixture and mix to make a soft dough. Knead lightly on a floured surface and cut into four pieces. Wrap each in plastic food wrap and chill for 3 hours.

3 Preheat oven to 180°C (350°F/ Gas 4). Roll out one piece of dough at a time to 5mm (¼in) thick and cut into desired shapes.

Brush shapes with egg white. Decorate cookies as desired.

4 Arrange cookies on lightly greased and floured baking sheets and bake for 10-12 minutes or until cookies are firm and edges are golden. Cool on wire racks and store in airtight containers.

5 To make icing, if using, stir together icing sugar, water and flavouring until smooth. Tint with colouring, if using, and pipe or spread over baked, cooled plain biscuits. Quickly add decorations before icing sets.

Makes 48

Kitchen Tip

To make coloured sugars or coconut place 60g (2oz) sugar or coconut in a covered container, add 2-3 drops desired food colouring, cover and shake until evenly coloured.

Christmas Mince Pies (page 12), Zimtsterne, Speculaas

Zimtsterne

200g (6½oz) icing sugar, sifted
200g (6½oz) ground almonds
60g (2oz) sugar
squeeze lemon juice
2 egg whites

1 Preheat oven to 180°C (350°F/ Gas 4). Stir together icing sugar, almonds, sugar, lemon juice and egg whites to the consistency of short pastry.

2 Place dough between sheets of plastic food wrap and roll out to 5mm (¼in) thick. Cut out shapes using a star-shaped cutter and place on paper-lined baking sheets.

3 Bake for 10 minutes or until golden. Cool on wire racks.

Makes 50-60

Speculaas

60g (2oz) dark soft brown sugar
1 tblspn milk
125g (4oz) plain flour, sifted
½ tspn ground cloves
½ tspn ground cinnamon
¼ tspn ground nutmeg
¼ tspn ground ginger
pinch salt
pinch baking powder
125g (4oz) butter, cubed
1 tblspn finely chopped almonds
1 tblspn finely chopped candied peel

1 Dissolve sugar in milk in a small saucepan over low heat. Cool. Sift together flour, spices, salt and baking powder. Rub in butter until mixture resembles breadcrumbs. Add milk mixture, almonds and peel, mix well to form a dough, then knead until pliable and no longer sticky. Wrap and chill for 30 minutes.

2 Preheat oven to 180°C (350°F/ Gas 4). Roll out dough to 5mm (¼in) thick, cut out Christmas shapes and place on lightly greased baking sheets. Bake for 10 minutes or until pale golden. Cool on wire racks.

Makes 14-18

Apricot Balls

220g (7oz) dried apricots

185g (6oz) desiccated coconut

185ml (6fl oz) canned sweetened condensed milk

1 tspn almond essence

icing sugar to coat

Place apricots in a food processor and process to finely chop. Transfer to a bowl, add coconut, condensed milk and almond essence and mix to combine. Shape mixture into 2cm (3/4in) balls and roll in icing sugar. Cover and chill until firm.

Makes 48

Pickled Eggs

500ml (16fl oz) white vinegar

250ml (8fl oz) water

1 tspn salt

1 tspn mixed pickling spice

1/2 tspn celery seeds

3 tblspn sugar

12 hard-boiled eggs

2 cloves garlic, crushed

1 Place vinegar, water, salt, pickling spice, celery seeds and sugar in a large saucepan. Bring to the boil, reduce heat and simmer for 5 minutes. Cool.

2 Shell the eggs and place in a clean, wide-mouthed jar. Strain pickling liquid over eggs and add garlic. Cover tightly and store in refrigerator for at least 3 days before serving.

Makes 12

Spiced Fruits

Prepare a week ahead, as the fruit improves in flavour. Store, covered, in refrigerator.

440g (14oz) can apricot halves

2 x 440g (14oz) cans peach halves

1/2 tspn whole cloves

1 stick cinnamon

8 whole allspice

60ml (2fl oz) white vinegar

125g (4oz) sugar

2 oranges, sliced

extra cloves, optional

Drain apricots and reserve syrup. Measure syrup and add enough liquid from peaches to make up to 250ml (8fl oz). Drain peaches. Place cloves, cinnamon stick, allspice, reserved syrup, vinegar, sugar and orange slices into a saucepan and bring to the boil. Add fruit and simmer for 5 minutes. Cool, then chill. If liked, stud fruit with extra cloves before cooking.

Makes 1.2 litres (2pt)

Irish Cream Liqueur

This is an excellent substitute for the famous commercial brand.

410g (13oz) can condensed milk

315ml (10fl oz) double cream

1/2 tspn coconut essence

3 eggs

2 tblspn chocolate sauce

375ml (12fl oz) whisky

Whisk together condensed milk, cream, coconut essence and eggs. Stir in chocolate sauce and whisky. Pour into sterilised bottles and refrigerate – will keep for up to 2 months.

Makes 1 litre (1 3/4pt)

Brandied Cherries

This gift improves with keeping.

500ml (16fl oz) water

375g (12oz) sugar

cinnamon sticks

1kg (2lb) large dark cherries, stoned

brandy

1 Place water, sugar and 1 cinnamon stick in a saucepan and bring to the boil. Reduce heat and simmer for 10 minutes. Add cherries and simmer for 5 minutes. Using a slotted spoon, remove cherries to warmed sterilised jars. Add a piece of cinnamon stick to each jar, if liked.

2 Boil syrup until reduced and thickened. Half-fill jars with syrup, then top up with brandy. Seal jars and store in a cool place.

Makes 1kg (2lb)

Cranberry Ginger Relish

This relish is a delicious accompaniment to the Christmas bird and can also be made with fresh or frozen redcurrants.

500g (1lb) fresh or frozen cranberries

1 tblspn finely grated orange rind

185ml (6fl oz) fresh orange juice

170g (5 1/2oz) honey or 125ml (4fl oz) pure maple syrup

2 tblspn finely chopped fresh ginger

Place all ingredients in a large saucepan and bring to the boil over medium heat. Reduce heat and gently simmer, stirring occasionally, for 10-15 minutes or until berries pop open. Cool. Store in covered jars in refrigerator for at least 1 week to allow flavours to mature.

Makes 750g (1 1/2lb)

Cheese and Herbs in Oil

250g (8oz) fresh cream cheese, feta or goat's cheese
sprigs of fresh thyme
black peppercorns
olive oil

Using two small spoons, shape soft cheese into small balls, or cut cheese into large cubes. Arrange in a sterilised glass jar with thyme and a few peppercorns. Cover with oil, seal and store in the refrigerator.

Makes 250g (8oz)

Homemade Mayonnaise

2 egg yolks
1/2 tspn salt
1 tspn French mustard
315ml (10fl oz) olive oil
2 tspn vinegar or lemon juice
freshly ground black pepper

1 Place egg yolks, salt and mustard in a bowl. Beat vigorously with a wooden spoon until thickened. Add oil, drop by drop, until 60ml (2fl oz) has been added. Stir in half the vinegar or lemon juice.

2 Gradually add remaining oil in a thin stream, beating constantly. Stir in remaining vinegar or lemon juice and season to taste with black pepper. If too thin, add 1-2 tablespoons hot water, beating well.

3 Pour mayonnaise into a sterilised jar. Cover and store in the refrigerator for 1-2 weeks.

Makes about 375ml (12fl oz)

Kitchen Tip
To make mayonnaise using a food processor, use 1 whole egg instead of 2 egg yolks and make in the same way, adding the oil in a slow steady stream with the motor running.

Beetroot Horseradish Pickle

Store in refrigerator for 8-10 days to allow flavours to develop before eating.

1kg (2lb) beetroot, cooked and cooled
60g (2oz) horseradish relish
125g (4oz) sugar
625ml (1pt) wine vinegar
1 tspn salt
1/2 tspn mustard seeds
6 juniper berries

1 Peel beetroot. If they are large, cut into wedges, if small leave whole. Mix together beetroot and horseradish relish and pack into hot, sterilised jars.

2 Place sugar, vinegar, salt, mustard seeds and juniper berries into a saucepan, bring to simmering and simmer for 15 minutes. Pour hot mixture over beetroot and seal.

Makes 1kg (2lb)

Pesto

4 cloves garlic
1 large bunch fresh basil, leaves only
8 tblspn roughly chopped fresh parsley
2 tblspn pine nuts or walnuts
90g (3oz) freshly grated Parmesan cheese
375ml (12fl oz) olive oil
freshly ground black pepper

1 Place garlic, basil, parsley, pine nuts or walnuts and Parmesan cheese in a food processor or blender and process until smooth. Gradually add oil processing until smooth and thick. Season to taste with black pepper.

2 Pack pesto into small sterilised jars and cover with a thin layer of olive oil before sealing. Keep refrigerated.

Makes 375ml (12fl oz)

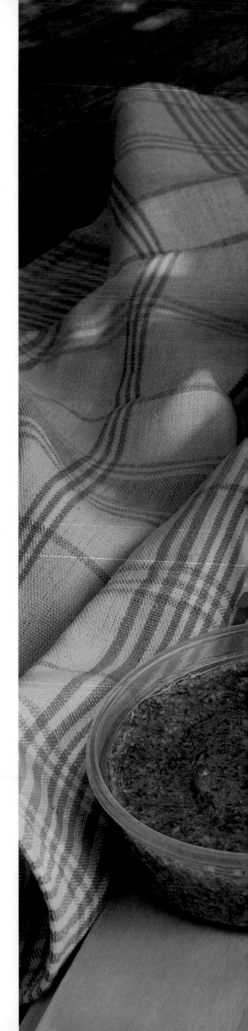

Cheese and Herbs in Oil, Homemade Mayonnaise, Pesto, Beetroot Horseradish Pickle

FESTIVE HOLIDAY DINING

As well as the traditional golden roast turkey and all the trimmings, this chapter includes lots of alternative but no less delicious ideas for festive fare.

Duck à L'Orange

2 x 2.5kg (5lb) ducks

peeled rind of 1 orange

salt and freshly ground black pepper

Orange Sauce

4 tblspn sugar

60ml (2fl oz) vinegar

375ml (12fl oz) duck stock (see Kitchen Tip this page)

1½ tblspn arrowroot blended with 2 tblspn port

rind of 2 oranges, shredded

125ml (4fl oz) port

2 tblspn orange-flavoured liqueur

1 tblspn butter

1 Preheat oven to 220°C (425°F/ Gas 7). Remove excess fat from ducks, place orange rind into cavities and season to taste. Truss and place, breast-side-up, in a roasting tin.

2 Bake for 20 minutes or until ducks brown and release some fat. Pour off fat. Reduce oven temperature to 190°C (375°F/Gas 5) and roast for 1 hour or until cooked.

3 To make sauce, stir sugar and vinegar in a saucepan over high heat to make a thick syrup. Remove from heat and gradually stir in stock until smooth. Return to heat and bring to the boil. Add arrowroot mixture and orange rind and simmer until sauce thickens. Remove from heat.

4 Keep ducks warm. Remove fat from roasting tin, leaving juices in the bottom. Place tin over moderate heat, stir in port and simmer until liquid reduces by half. Strain juices into orange sauce, bring to simmering and stir in liqueur. Season to taste, add butter and stir until melted.

5 Cut birds into serving portions, arrange on serving plates and glaze with some of the sauce. Serve remaining sauce separately.

Serves 8

Kitchen Tip
To make duck stock, heat a little oil in a saucepan and brown the neck and giblets of the ducks. Pour off all fat and add 500ml (16fl oz) water, a bouquet garni and gently simmer for 1 hour. Strain stock before using.

Saffron Rice

60g (2oz) ghee

1 tspn cumin seeds

1 cinnamon stick

5 cloves

4-5 cardamom pods

1 small onion, finely chopped

440g (14oz) long-grain rice

salt and freshly ground black pepper

1 litre (1¾pt) hot chicken stock

½ tspn saffron threads

3 tblspn slivered almonds, toasted

1 Melt ghee in a saucepan over low heat, add cumin, cinnamon, cloves and cardamom and cook for 3 minutes. Add onion and cook until soft. Stir in rice and season.

2 Combine hot stock and saffron, stir into rice and bring to the boil. Cover tightly, reduce heat and simmer for 18-20 minutes or until all liquid is absorbed and rice is tender. Uncover and stand rice over heat for 1-2 minutes. Sprinkle with almonds and serve.

Serves 8

Duck à L'Orange, Saffron Rice, Christmas Pudding (page 18)

Festive Poached Salmon

Festive Poached Salmon

Garnish this special fish dish with a sprig of holly and serve with boiled new potatoes and a tossed green salad.

1.5kg (3lb) whole fresh salmon

red and green peppers, cut in fine julienne strips

bottled or homemade vinaigrette dressing

Court Bouillon

750ml (1¹/4pt) water or half white wine, half water

1 tblspn vinegar

1 onion, sliced

5-6 fresh parsley sprigs, a sprig of thyme and a bay leaf

6 black peppercorns

1 tspn salt

Aioli

2 cloves garlic, finely chopped

250g (8oz) Homemade Mayonnaise (page 26)

Mango Mint Sauce

1 fresh mango or 220g (7oz) canned sliced mango, drained

1 tblspn white wine vinegar

1 tblspn chopped fresh mint

2 tblspn olive oil

Remoulade

1 tblspn capers

1 tblspn finely chopped gherkins

250g (8oz) Homemade Mayonnaise (page 26)

2 tblspn Dijon mustard

1 tblspn chopped fresh parsley

1 To make bouillon, place ingredients in a saucepan — if using white wine omit the vinegar. Bring to the boil and simmer for 10 minutes. Pour into a baking dish just large enough to hold fish.

2 Preheat oven to 160°C (325°F/ Gas 3). Place fish on a rack in dish, cover with foil or baking paper and bake, basting every 15 minutes, for 30-35 minutes or until cooked.

3 Lift salmon from bouillon, cool slightly and remove the skin, leaving head and tail intact. Place on a serving plate, cover loosely and chill until ready to serve.

4 To make Aioli, stir garlic into mayonnaise. To make mango sauce, purée mango flesh in a food processor with vinegar and mint. Gradually whisk in oil. To make Remoulade, fold capers and gherkins into mayonnaise. Stir in mustard and parsley. Chill sauces until ready to serve.

5 Drop red and green peppers into boiling water for 30 seconds, drain and toss with little vinaigrette. Spoon mixture along length of fish. Serve fish at room temperature with the three sauces.

Serves 8-10

Guinness Glazed Ham

Delicious served with Spiced Fruits (page 25).

7.5kg (15lb) cooked leg of ham
500ml (16fl oz) Guinness or stout
170g (5^1/$_2$oz) soft brown sugar
1 tblspn dry mustard
1 tspn ground ginger
2 tspn ground cardamom
watercress or parsley for garnish

1 Preheat oven to 160°C (325°F/ Gas 3). Skin ham, leaving a portion of skin around the bone. Place ham, fat-side-up, in a roasting tin and pour over 440ml (14fl oz) of the stout. Bake for 3 hours, basting occasionally with stout. Remove ham from oven and baste thoroughly with drippings to glaze.

2 Increase oven temperature to 200°C (400°F/Gas 6). Combine sugar, mustard, ginger, cardamom and enough remaining stout to make a paste. Spread mixture over ham and bake for 35 minutes or until well glazed. Garnish with watercress or parsley and serve.

Serves 20-30

Thai Roast Pork

2kg (4lb) pork loin, neck or rolled boned shoulder
2 tspn ground cumin
6 cloves garlic, crushed with a little salt
freshly ground black pepper
1 pineapple
4 tblspn soy sauce
60ml (2fl oz) vinegar
6 tblspn brown sugar
6 tblspn chopped fresh coriander

1 Remove skin from pork – it can be baked separately in a hot oven if you want crackling.

Combine cumin, garlic and black pepper to taste and rub into pork.

2 Preheat oven to 180°C (350°F/ Gas 4). Cut peel from pineapple and use some of it to cover pork. Place pork in a baking dish and bake for 1½ hours or until almost tender. Remove from oven and discard pineapple peel.

3 Combine soy sauce, vinegar and sugar and brush some over pork. Return to oven and bake, basting frequently with remaining mixture, for 15 minutes or until pork is cooked.

4 Remove pork to a platter, skim fat from pan juices and serve juice with the meat. Cut peeled pineapple into rings or spears and use with coriander to garnish pork.

Serves 8

Thai Roast Pork

Roast Goose with Nut Stuffing

Order a young goose — after 10 months, the flesh may be tough. If you prefer your goose cold with salad, omit the stuffing and roast it the day before with a quartered onion and apple in the cavity to flavour.

1 x 4-5kg (8-10lb) goose, cleaned

1 litre (1³/₄pt) stock made with neck and giblets, see Kitchen Tip page 28 for making duck stock

Nut Stuffing

60g (2oz) butter

2 onions, finely chopped

4 stalks celery, chopped

3 tart apples, chopped

¹/₂ tspn dried thyme

¹/₂ tspn dried sage

2 tspn finely grated lemon rind

250g (8oz) breadcrumbs, made from stale bread

125g (4oz) chopped pecans or walnuts

salt and freshly ground black pepper

1 To make stuffing, melt butter in a frying pan over a moderate heat and fry onions and celery until soft. Remove from heat and combine with apples, herbs, lemon rind, breadcrumbs and nuts. Season to taste.

2 Preheat oven to 200°C (400°F/ Gas 6). Season goose with salt and black pepper. Place on a rack in roasting tin and roast for 20 minutes. Drain off all fat. Fill cavity with stuffing, secure opening and tie legs loosely together.

3 Reduce oven to 180°C (350°F/ Gas 4). Turn goose over so that it is breast-side-down on rack. Add 500ml (16fl oz) stock to tin, cover bird with a tent of foil, sealing to edge of tin and roast for 2 hours, basting occasionally and adding more stock as needed. Remove foil and turn bird breast-side-up. Roast for 20-30 minutes longer or until skin is crisp and goose is cooked. Transfer to a serving platter, cover and stand for 15 minutes before carving.

4 Spoon off all fat from roasting juices. Add remaining stock to juices, heat to boiling and boil until reduced and thickened slightly. Adjust seasoning and strain gravy into sauce boat. Serve with goose. For a special touch, bake tartlet shells the night before (or order them from your cake shop) and fill with Cranberry Ginger Relish (page 25) or redcurrant jelly and serve with the goose.

Serves 6-8

French Roast Stuffed Turkey

Turkey Stock

turkey giblets and neck

1 onion, halved

1 bay leaf

1 stalk celery

1.8 litres (3pt) water

1 x 6kg (12lb) turkey

1 quantity Forcemeat Stuffing with Pecans (page 34)

1 quantity Herbed Bread Stuffing (recipe follows)

60g (2oz) butter, softened

salt and freshly ground black pepper

Gravy

30g (1oz) butter

2 tblspn plain flour

1 To make stock, place turkey giblets and neck, onion, bay leaf, celery and water in a large saucepan and simmer until liquid reduces to 1.2 litres (2pt). Strain.

2 Preheat oven to 180°C (350°F/ Gas 4). Carefully loosen skin from neck area and breast and loosely fill with forcemeat stuffing. Press outside of breast to mould into shape, secure neck skin to back with skewers and tuck wings under body. Spoon bread stuffing into body cavity. Secure tail opening and tie legs close to body. Wipe bird dry, spread with butter and season to taste with salt and black pepper.

3 Place turkey on rack in roasting tin, add 500ml (16fl oz) of the stock, cover tin tightly with foil and roast, basting every 20-25 minutes, for 3¹/₂-4 hours or until juices run clear when thigh is pierced with a skewer. Remove foil for the last 30 minutes of cooking to allow turkey to brown. Transfer turkey to a heated platter, cover and stand for 15 minutes before carving.

4 To make gravy, pour off all but 3 tablespoons fat from roasting juices. Place tin over low heat, stir in butter and flour and stir until brown. Blend in 500ml (16fl oz) stock. Bring to the boil, reduce heat and simmer until thickened, adding remaining stock, if needed. Strain gravy and serve with turkey.

Serves 8-10

Herbed Bread Stuffing

8 spring onions, finely chopped, including some green tops

30g (1oz) butter

125g (4oz) breadcrumbs, made from stale bread

2 tblspn snipped fresh chives

1 tblspn chopped mixed fresh herbs (thyme, marjoram, sage)

1 tspn finely grated lemon rind

1 egg, beaten

salt and freshly ground black pepper

lemon juice or stock

Combine spring onions, butter, breadcrumbs, herbs and lemon rind, cover and store in the refrigerator until ready to use. Add egg, season to taste with salt and black pepper and add a little lemon juice or stock to moisten. Toss with a fork; do not overmix. Use as directed in French Roast Stuffed Turkey (recipe this page).

Bread Sauce, Bourbon Sweet Potatoes (page 34); French Roast Stuffed Turkey

Forcemeat Stuffing with Pecans

This stuffing can be made using just pork mince, if you wish.

375g (12oz) lean pork mince

375g (12oz) lean veal mince

90g (3oz) breadcrumbs, made from stale bread

1 tblspn chopped mixed fresh herbs such as parsley, thyme, sage

1-2 onions, finely chopped

60g (2oz) bacon, finely chopped

1 egg, beaten

90g (3oz) pecans, toasted and roughly chopped

1 tspn finely grated lemon rind

salt and freshly ground black pepper

Combine all ingredients and mix well, seasoning to taste with salt and black pepper. Use as directed in French Roast Stuffed Turkey (page 32).

Bourbon Sweet Potatoes

1kg (2lb) orange sweet potatoes, peeled and cut into even-sized pieces

60g (2oz) butter

1 tblspn vegetable oil

1 tblspn honey

2 tblspn bourbon or whisky

pinch ground ginger

1 Preheat oven to 180°C (350°F/ Gas 4). Cook sweet potatoes in a large saucepan of boiling salted water for 5 minutes. Drain. Melt half the butter with oil in a baking dish and stir in honey, bourbon or whisky and ginger. Add sweet potatoes and toss in mixture to coat.

2 Bake for 40 minutes, brushing with honey mixture and turning occasionally, until potatoes are tender.

Serves 8

Bread Sauce

250ml (8fl oz) milk

1 onion, chopped

1 bay leaf

6 black peppercorns

60g (2oz) white breadcrumbs, made from stale bread

1/2 tspn salt

1 tspn butter

extra breadcrumbs, fried in extra butter

1 Place milk, onion, bay leaf and peppercorns in a small saucepan over a moderate heat and simmer for 3 minutes. Strain and return to saucepan.

2 Add breadcrumbs and salt to milk and simmer, stirring, until sauce is creamy. Stir in butter, pour into a sauce boat and sprinkle with buttered crumbs. Serve immediately.

Makes about 375ml (12fl oz)

Roast Rib of Beef

1 standing rib roast (6 or more ribs)

salt and freshly ground black pepper

Herbed Piquant Sauce

5-6 spring onions, finely chopped

1 very small clove garlic, chopped

3 tblspn dry white wine

1 tblspn wine vinegar

250g (8oz) butter, softened

1 tblspn each chopped fresh parsley and chervil or chives

1 tspn lemon juice

1 tspn salt

freshly ground black pepper

ground nutmeg

1 Preheat oven to 220°C (425°F/ Gas 7). Rub roast all over with salt and black pepper. Place on a rack, fat-side-up, in a roasting tin and roast for 20 minutes.

2 Reduce oven temperature to 180°C (350°F/Gas 4) and roast until cooked as desired – about 30 minutes per 1kg (2lb) for rare; about 1 hour per 1kg (2lb) for well

done. Baste every 30 minutes with pan juices. Remove from oven and stand, covered with foil, for 15 minutes to allow juices to settle.

3 To make sauce, place spring onions, garlic, wine and vinegar in a small saucepan. Bring to the boil and boil for 2 minutes or until reduced to 1 tablespoon. Cool slightly, then gradually whisk in butter until blended and creamy, like mayonnaise. Stir in herbs, lemon juice, salt and black pepper and nutmeg to taste. Place in a sauce boat and set in a pan of warm water to keep warm.

4 To serve, place beef, fat-side-down, on a carving board and remove ribs by cutting close down the line of bones. Cut ribs apart and set aside. Turn roast upright and carve slices from one end, arranging them around the roast for serving. Serve beef with the ribs, pan juices and sauce.

Serves 6-8

Salad of Duck with Wild Rice

2 x 2.5kg (5lb) ducks

salt

500g (1lb) pitted cherries or sliced fresh peaches

250ml (8fl oz) orange juice

60g (2oz) sugar

500g (1lb) sugar snap peas, green beans or mangetout

3 large oranges, rind and pith removed

155g (5oz) wild rice

220g (7oz) basmati rice

Raspberry Vinaigrette

90ml (3fl oz) olive oil

60ml (2fl oz) raspberry vinegar

1 tblspn sour cream

1 Preheat oven to 220°C (425°F/ Gas 7). Remove excess fat from ducks, wipe dry and rub inside and out with salt. Place, breast-side-up, in a roasting tin. Bake for 20 minutes. Reduce oven temperature to 190°C (375°F/Gas 5) and roast for 40-60 minutes longer or until cooked. Cool ducks, cut off

Salad of Duck with Wild Rice

wings, thighs and legs and reserve for another meal. Cut breasts into thin slices.

2 Place cherries or peaches, orange juice and sugar in a saucepan and bring to the boil, stirring to dissolve sugar. Cool. Boil, steam or microwave peas, beans or mangetout until just tender, drain and refresh in cold water. Cut oranges into thin slices. To make vinaigrette, whisk all ingredients together until thickened.

3 Cook wild rice and basmati rice, separately, following packet directions. Drain and cool. Combine rices and toss with half the vinaigrette.

4 To assemble, spoon rice along one side of a large platter or individual plates. Arrange duck over rice, place peas, beans or mangetout down one side, and garnish with orange slices, cherries or peaches and watercress. Drizzle with remaining vinaigrette and serve.

Serves 4-6

Chutney-glazed Poussin

6 x 500g (1lb) poussin

fresh parsley or watercress for garnish

Pine Nut Stuffing

3 spring onions, finely chopped

90g (3oz) unsalted butter

185g (6oz) diced stale bread

1 stalk celery, finely chopped

90g (3oz) sultanas

30g (1oz) pine nuts, chopped

2 tspn finely chopped fresh sage or 1/2 teaspoon dried sage

1 tspn finely grated orange rind

1 tspn finely grated lemon rind

salt and freshly ground black pepper

125ml (4fl oz) dry white wine or orange juice

Mango Chutney Glaze

60g (2oz) sugar

1 tblspn white wine vinegar

125ml (4fl oz) fresh orange juice

rind of 1/2 orange, cut into thin strips

60g (2oz) mango chutney

1 Preheat oven to 200°C (400°F/ Gas 6). To make stuffing, cook spring onions in 60g (2oz) of the butter in a frying pan over low heat for 5 minutes. Remove from the heat and stir in remaining stuffing ingredients, mixing well.

2 Pat poussin dry. Loosely pack stuffing into cavities of birds. Truss into neat shapes, sprinkle with salt and black pepper and place on a rack in a roasting tin. Melt remaining butter, brush over birds and roast for 30 minutes.

3 To make glaze, dissolve sugar and vinegar in a small non-reactive saucepan over moderate heat and cook until a pale amber in colour. Remove from heat, stir in orange juice and rind, return to heat and cook, stirring, until smooth. Stir in chutney.

4 Reduce oven to 180°C (350°F/ Gas 4) and roast birds for 15 minutes. Brush with glaze and roast, brushing with glaze, every 10 minutes, for 30 minutes longer or until cooked and well glazed. Garnish with parsley or watercress.

Serves 12

Turkey Salad with Cranberry Vinaigrette

Turkey Salad with Cranberry Vinaigrette

assorted salad greens, washed and crisped

750g (1¹/₂lb) cooked smoked turkey, sliced

300g (9¹/₂oz) cherry tomatoes

90g (3oz) pecans, toasted

Cranberry Vinaigrette

1 clove garlic, finely chopped

1 tspn wholegrain mustard

1 tblspn balsamic vinegar

2 tblspn canned, preserved cranberries

125ml (4fl oz) virgin olive oil

salt and freshly ground black pepper

1 Arrange salad greens on six serving plates and top with turkey, tomatoes and pecans.

2 To make vinaigrette, whisk together garlic, mustard, vinegar and cranberries, gradually adding oil, until combined and slightly thickened. Season to taste with salt and black pepper. Drizzle over salads.

Serves 6

Old English Stilton Soup

Rich and delicious for a traditional Christmas dinner.

30g (1oz) butter

2 tblspn plain flour

1.2 litres (2pt) chicken stock

185g (6oz) Stilton cheese

250ml (8fl oz) double cream

185ml (6fl oz) double cream, whipped

3 tblspn chopped fresh parsley or chives

1 Melt butter in saucepan over moderate heat, add flour and stir for 1 minute. Remove from heat, gradually stir in stock until smooth. Return to heat and cook, stirring constantly, until slightly thickened.

2 Mash cheese with a fork, then beat in 250ml (8fl oz) cream until blended. Whisk mixture into soup and bring to the boil. Serve in soup plates or bowls garnished with a spoonful of whipped cream sprinkled with parsley or chives.

Serves 8

Quail with Grapes

Serve these elegant little birds on a bed of Saffron Rice (page 28) and ensure that each person has a finger bowl.

12 quail
salt and freshly ground black pepper
90g (3oz) butter
250ml (8fl oz) dry white wine
2-3 tblspn freshly squeezed lemon juice
125g (4oz) green seedless grapes, stalks removed

1 Pat birds dry and season with salt and black pepper to taste. Melt butter in a shallow flameproof casserole or large frying pan over a moderate heat and cook quail until golden on all sides.

2 Add wine and lemon juice, cover and simmer gently over low heat for 15 minutes. Add grapes and cook for 5-10 minutes longer or until birds are cooked.

3 Remove quail to a heated platter and keep warm. Simmer cooking juices in casserole until reduced and slightly thick, pour over birds and serve immediately.

Serves 6-8

Party Fish Salad

250ml (8fl oz) water
1 onion, sliced
1 stalk celery, sliced
1 bay leaf
1 tspn salt
1 x 2kg (4lb) whole white fish or 1.5kg (3lb) fish fillets
1 pineapple, peeled and cut into chunks
4-6 spring onions, finely chopped with some green tops
250g (8oz) Homemade Mayonnaise, (page 26)
8-10 mangetout, blanched
2 tblspn chopped fresh parsley
1 lemon, cut into thin wedges

1 Preheat oven to 180°C (350°F/ Gas 4). Place water, onion, celery, bay leaf and salt in a large saucepan, bring to the boil, reduce heat and simmer for 5 minutes. Strain stock into a baking dish just large enough to hold fish. Add fish, cover with foil and bake whole fish for 35 minutes; fillets for 15 minutes, or until just tender.

2 Remove from heat, lift fish from stock and cool slightly. Break into small flakes, removing any bones and skin, and place in a bowl. Add pineapple and spring onions and fold in mayonnaise. Chill until ready to serve.

3 Spoon fish mixture onto a serving dish, garnish with mangetout, parsley and lemon wedges.

Serves 8-10

Party Fish Salad

COME FOR A CUPPA

Treat your holiday guests and visitors to a selection of these mouthwatering desserts, delicate tea sandwiches and sweet sensations. They're sure to come back for more!

Cucumber Sandwiches

1-2 cucumbers
vinegar or lemon juice
salt
softened butter
1 loaf brown bread, very thinly sliced

1 Peel and cut cucumbers into very thin transparent slices. Place in a bowl, sprinkle with a little vinegar or lemon juice and salt and set aside for 30 minutes. Drain off excess juices.

2 Butter bread slices and cover half of them with two layers of cucumber. Top with remaining bread, buttered-side-down. Press firmly, wrap and chill for 1 hour.

3 Trim crusts and cut each sandwich into three rectangles. Place on a serving plate and cover with a lightly dampened cloth until ready to serve.

Serves 6-8

Watercress Sandwiches

softened butter
rough rye or brown bread, very thinly sliced
watercress, cleaned and crisped

Butter bread slices and pile half of them high with watercress. Press another slice of bread, buttered-side-down, on top until the contents creak. Trim crusts and cut sandwiches in half but not quarters – the dark green leaves burst out at the seams.

The Ritz's Egg Sandwiches

5 hard-boiled eggs, shelled
dash Tabasco sauce, optional
1 loaf white bread, very thinly sliced and buttered
watercress

Mayonnaise

2 egg yolks
2 tspn dry English mustard
1 tblspn Worcestershire sauce
1/2 tspn salt
1/4 tspn ground white pepper
220ml (7fl oz) olive oil
1 tblspn lemon juice

1 To make mayonnaise, place egg yolks, mustard, Worcestershire sauce, salt and white pepper in a bowl and whisk to combine. Continue to whisk vigorously, adding a few drops of oil at a time, until all oil is used and mixture is thick. Add lemon juice to taste.

2 Roughly chop hard-boiled eggs and stir into mayonnaise. Season to taste with Tabasco (if using). Spread mixture on half the buttered bread slices, top with watercress and remaining bread slices. Press firmly, wrap and chill for 1 hour. Trim crusts and cut each sandwich into three rectangles.

Serves 8

The Ritz's Egg, Cucumber and Watercress Sandwiches, Éclairs, Fruit Tarts, Brandy Snaps (page 41)

Ham and Herb Cheese Ribbons

softened butter

1 loaf brown bread, thinly sliced

1 loaf white bread, thinly sliced

375g (12oz) ham, finely chopped

Herb Cheese Filling

250g (8oz) cream cheese, softened

1 tblspn lemon juice

freshly ground black pepper

3 tblspn chopped mixed fresh herbs such as chives, thyme, marjoram, oregano

4-6 tblspn finely chopped fresh parsley

4 spring onions, finely chopped

1 To make filling, beat cream cheese with lemon juice and black pepper to taste until smooth. Stir in herbs and spring onions.

2 Butter bread slices. Spread one slice with cheese filling, top with a slice of bread of the other colour, buttered-side-down, then butter upper side of this slice. Cover with ham and top with a slice of bread of the first colour.

3 Wrap in plastic food wrap then pack into airtight containers and refrigerate. To serve, trim crusts and cut each sandwich into three finger lengths.

Serves 25

Eclairs

250ml (8fl oz) double cream, whipped

Choux Pastry

315ml (10fl oz) water

60g (2oz) butter

125g (4oz) plain flour, sifted

1 tblspn caster sugar

3 large eggs

Créme Patissière

2 medium eggs

60g (2oz) sugar

4 tblspn plain flour, sifted

315ml (10fl oz) milk

60g (2oz) semi-sweet chocolate, melted, optional

Chocolate and Coffee Icings

125g (4oz) semi-sweet chocolate, melted and warm

155g (5oz) icing sugar, sifted

1 tspn instant coffee powder

1 scant tblspn boiling water

1 To make pastry, heat water and butter in a saucepan to boiling point, add flour and stir over moderate heat until mixture leaves sides of pan. Stir in sugar and cool to lukewarm. Beat in eggs, one at a time, until dough is smooth and satiny.

2 Preheat oven to 200°C (400°F/ Gas 6). Pipe dough through a 1cm (1/2in) nozzle into 6cm (2 1/2in) lengths onto greased baking sheets and bake for 40 minutes. Place pastries onto wire racks and, while still warm, slit down one side to allow steam to escape.

3 To make Créme Patissiere, beat eggs and sugar until creamy. Stir in flour and enough of the milk to make a smooth thick paste. Scald remaining milk, then gradually stir into egg mixture. Transfer mixture to saucepan, bring almost to the boil and cook, stirring constantly, for 5 minutes. Remove from the heat and stir in 60g (2oz) chocolate (if using). Cover and cool.

4 To glaze with chocolate icing, pour melted chocolate into a shallow bowl. Carefully dip tops of half the éclairs into chocolate and allow to set. To make coffee icing, place icing sugar, coffee powder and water in a bowl and mix to combine. Stir over hot water until melted and smooth. Spread over remaining éclairs and allow to set.

5 To fill éclairs, gently prise pastries open and pipe a narrow line of Créme Patissiere along one inside surface and a line of whipped cream along the other.

Makes 24-28

Fruit Tarts

500g (1lb) strawberries or raspberries or other delicate fruit

4 tblspn seedless strawberry jam or redcurrant jelly

60ml (2fl oz) water

Pastry

125g (4oz) plain flour

pinch salt

1 tblspn caster sugar

60g (2oz) butter

1 egg, beaten

Liqueur Cream Filling

1/2 quantity plain Créme Patissiere (see Eclairs recipe this page)

2 tspn liqueur of your choice

170ml (5 1/2fl oz) double cream, whipped

1 To make pastry, sift together flour and salt, make a well in centre, add sugar, butter and egg and work mixture with fingers to make a firm dough, adding a few drops water to bind. Knead until smooth, wrap and chill for 1 hour.

2 Preheat oven to 190°C (375°F/ Gas 5). Roll dough out thinly on a lightly floured surface, cut out ten 8.5cm (3 1/2in) circles and use to line greased 6cm (2 1/2in) shallow patty tins, pressing well into tins. Bake for 18 minutes or until pale and golden. Turn out of tins to cool.

3 To make filling, prepare Créme Patissiere and set aside to cool. Stir in liqueur then whipped cream. Cover and chill until required. To serve, pipe cream into pastry cases and cover with fruit. Heat jam or jelly with water until smooth and thickened, cool slightly and brush over fruit.

Makes 10

Iced Plum Cream in Wafer Cups

Brandy Snaps

60g (2oz) butter

60g (2oz) soft light brown sugar

125g (4oz) golden syrup

1 tspn ground ginger

60g (2oz) plain flour, sifted

2 tspn finely grated lemon rind

2 tspn lemon juice

whipped double cream to fill

1 Preheat oven to 220°C (425°F/ Gas 7). Place butter, sugar, golden syrup and ginger in a saucepan over low heat and stir until butter melts and sugar dissolves. Cool slightly, add flour, lemon rind and lemon juice and mix well.

2 Line two baking sheets with nonstick baking paper. Drop generous teaspoons of mixture in 5 mounds, 10cm (4in) apart, on one sheet and bake for 12-15 minutes or until mounds spread out to form lacey malleable rounds.

3 Cool briefly, remove with a palette knife and quickly roll around handle of a wooden spoon. Allow to set, then carefully slip off spoon and cool. While rolling one batch, bake the next. Store in an airtight container. Just prior to serving, fill with whipped cream.

Makes 16

Iced Plum Cream in Wafer Cups

60ml (2fl oz) orange-flavoured liqueur or rum

90g (3oz) diced pitted prunes

60g (2oz) chopped dried apricots

1 litre (1³/4pt) vanilla ice cream, slightly softened

Wafer Cups

60g (2oz) butter

75g (2¹/2oz) caster or brown sugar

125g (4oz) golden syrup

60g (2oz) plain flour, sifted

1 tspn ground ginger

30g (1oz) chopped walnuts or pecans

1 Heat liqueur or rum until warm, add prunes and apricots and soak for 30 minutes. Fold mixture into ice cream and pack into a freezerproof container. Cover and freeze until ready to serve.

2 To make cups, melt butter, sugar and golden syrup in a saucepan over low heat until combined. Cool to lukewarm. Stir in flour and ginger, then nuts.

3 Preheat oven to 180°C (350°F/ Gas 4). Grease two baking sheets. Drop 2-3 tablespoons of mixture on each tray, allowing room for spreading. Bake one tray at a time for 10 minutes or until golden, cool briefly then ease wafers from sheet with spatula.

4 Turn small moulds or cups upside down and working quickly, wrap each wafer, rough-side-out, over mould. Briefly hold until wafer sets then remove to a wire rack to cool. Continue with remaining mixture, alternating trays. Store in an airtight container. To serve, spoon plum cream into cups and serve immediately.

Serves 8-10

Coffee Rum Gâteau

Serve with poached apples, pears or any fruit in season.

185g (6oz) butter, softened

170g (5¹/₂oz) caster sugar

3 eggs, lightly beaten

185g (6oz) self-raising flour, sifted

¹/₂ tspn salt

315ml (10fl oz) strong black coffee

3 tblspn rum or brandy

300ml (9¹/₂fl oz) double cream, lightly whipped

toasted flaked almonds to decorate

1 Preheat oven to 180°C (350°F/ Gas 4). Beat butter until creamy, add sugar and beat until light and fluffy. Add eggs, one at a time, beating well. Fold in flour and salt, taking care not to overmix.

2 Turn mixture into a greased 20cm (8in) ring tin and bake for 25 minutes or until cake is cooked. Stand in tin for 5 minutes, then turn onto a wire rack to cool.

3 Return cake to clean tin. Combine coffee and rum and slowly pour over cake. Allow to steep for a few hours. Turn onto a serving plate, top with whipped cream and decorate with almonds. Chill until ready to serve.

Serves 6-8

Ginger Rum Ice Cream

Delicious served with Apple Mincemeat Tart (page 15).

2 litres (3¹/₂pt) vanilla ice cream, slightly softened

250g (8oz) preserved ginger in syrup, drained and finely sliced, syrup reserved

60ml (2fl oz) rum

1 The day before serving, turn ice cream into a large bowl and use a fork to mix in ginger and rum as quickly as possible to avoid melting. Return mixture to ice cream container, cover and freeze overnight.

2 Scoop into large balls and pile into a pretty serving bowl. Decorate if liked with a little extra sliced ginger and drizzle with ginger syrup.

Serves 8-10

Eggnog Pie

Crumb Crust

220g (7oz) semi-sweet biscuit crumbs

75g (2¹/₂oz) caster sugar

125g (4oz) butter, melted

Eggnog Filling

1¹/₂ tblspn gelatine

90ml (3fl oz) cold water

250ml (8fl oz) milk

4 large eggs, separated

185g (6oz) sugar

pinch salt

¹/₄ tspn freshly grated nutmeg

3 tblspn rum, whisky or brandy

1 tspn vanilla essence

185ml (6fl oz) double cream, whipped

extra whipped cream and nutmeg to decorate

1 Preheat oven to 200°C (400°F/ Gas 6). To make crust, combine biscuit crumbs, sugar and butter and press firmly over base and up sides of a 25cm (10in) flan tin with removable base. Bake for 5 minutes. Cool.

2 To make filling, sprinkle gelatine over water in a heatproof bowl. Scald milk. Beat egg yolks, half the sugar, salt and nutmeg until thick. Stir in a little hot milk, then stir this mixture back into remaining milk in saucepan.

3 Cook over low heat, stirring constantly, until mixture coats the spoon. Dip bottom of saucepan into cold water to stop cooking. Stir gelatine over hot water until melted, then stir into custard. Strain custard into a clean bowl, add rum, whisky or brandy and vanilla essence, cool, then chill until mixture is the consistency of unbeaten egg white.

4 Beat egg whites until foamy, gradually beat in remaining sugar until stiff peaks form. Fold meringue into custard mixture then fold in whipped cream. Spoon filling into crumb crust and chill until firm, preferably overnight. Just prior to serving, decorate with extra whipped cream and sprinkle with nutmeg.

Serves 8

Frozen Plum Pudding

Start this three days in advance of serving.

220g (7oz) mixed dried fruit

2 slices glacé pineapple, chopped

90g (3oz) red glacé cherries

125ml (4fl oz) brandy

1 litre (1³/₄pt) best quality chocolate ice cream, slightly softened

1 litre (1³/₄pt) best quality vanilla ice cream, slightly softened

125g (4oz) dark chocolate, grated

extra glacé fruit and whipped double cream to serve

1 Soak dried fruit, pineapple and cherries overnight in the brandy.

2 Turn ice creams into a large bowl and quickly stir in soaked fruit and chocolate. Pack mixture into a metal basin, cover tightly and freeze until firm, preferably overnight.

3 To remove, briefly dip basin in hot water and turn mould out onto a serving plate. Return to freezer until required (this is best done several hours ahead or overnight). Decorate with extra glacé fruit, cut in slices, and serve with whipped cream.

Serves 8-10

Pear and Brandy Gratin

4 egg yolks

125g (4oz) caster sugar

250ml (8fl oz) double cream, scalded

2 tblspn brandy

1/2 tspn ground ginger

4 almost-ripe pears, peeled, halved and cored

90ml (3fl oz) water

1 Beat egg yolks and 60g (2oz) sugar until pale. Gradually whisk hot cream into egg mixture. Return to saucepan and stir over low heat until thickened. Whisk until luke-warm. Stir in brandy and ginger, cover and set aside.

2 Preheat oven to 190°C (375°F/ Gas 5). Cut pears into 5mm (1/4in) slices, keeping slices together in the half-pear shape. Arrange, cut-side-down, in a buttered 25cm (10in) round ovenproof dish and open into fan shapes.

3 Add water to dish and sprinkle pears with remaining sugar. Bake until tender and lightly caramelised, covering with baking paper or foil if they colour too quickly. Pour custard over hot pears. Cook under a preheated medium grill for 2 minutes or until top is golden.

Serves 4-6

Hot Fruit Soufflés

2 apples, peeled, cored and chopped

1 pear, peeled, cored and chopped

90g (3oz) sugar

1 tblspn fruit-flavoured liqueur or brandy

1 tspn lemon juice

2 egg yolks

5 egg whites

pinch cream of tartar

sifted icing sugar to serve

1 Cook apples and pear, covered, in a heavy saucepan with a little water until very soft. Purée fruit and cook, stirring, until purée is very thick. Cool.

2 Stir sugar, liqueur and lemon juice into purée. Beat egg yolks until creamy and gradually stir in purée until combined. Set aside.

3 Preheat oven to 220°C (425°F/ Gas 7). Butter six individual soufflé dishes and coat insides with caster sugar. Beat egg whites with cream of tartar just until stiff peaks form. Stir 1 tablespoon of whites into fruit mixture, then quickly fold in remaining whites.

4 Spoon mixture into dishes, levelling tops with a spatula. Using a wet thumb make an indentation in the mixture, working around the inside edge of each soufflé dish, to help form a cap when soufflés are baked.

5 Reduce oven temperature to 190°C (375°F/Gas 5) and bake for 10 minutes or until soufflés are well-risen. Dust with icing sugar and serve immediately.

Serves 6

Hot Apple and Pear Soufflés

Demerara Chestnut Meringues

Demerara Chestnut Meringues

125g (4oz) demerara sugar

2 large egg whites

Chestnut Filling

60g (2oz) sugar

90ml (3fl oz) milk

220g (7oz) canned unsweetened chestnut purée

60g (2oz) dark chocolate, cut into small pieces

125ml (4fl oz) double cream, whipped

pieces of marron glacé and syrup, or shaved dark chocolate to decorate

extra double cream to serve

1 Preheat oven to 120°C (250°F/ Gas ¹/₂). Spread sugar on a baking sheet and place in oven for 1 hour to dry out. Cool. Place sugar in a blender or food processor and process to finely grind.

2 Beat egg whites to soft peaks. Beat in half the sugar until mixture is thick and shiny. Using a large metal spoon gently fold in remaining sugar. It's not necessary to mix thoroughly; if the mixture is overworked the meringue will break.

3 To shape meringues, use 2 damp dessertspoons. Use one to scoop up a heaped spoonful of meringue; the other to push off onto a paper-lined baking sheet, to form a half-egg shape. If necessary, neaten shapes with a knife dipped in cold water. Repeat with remaining mixture.

4 Sprinkle tops of meringues with a little extra sugar and bake for 1 hour or until firm. Gently lift each meringue and press base to make a hollow. Bake for 30 minutes longer or until crisp and dry. Turn off oven and allow to cool in oven.

5 To make filling, dissolve sugar in milk in a saucepan over low heat. Add chestnut purée and chocolate and stir until smooth. If lumpy, rub through a sieve. Cool completely, then fold in whipped cream.

6 To serve, scoop filling onto base of one meringue, sandwich with another meringue and place on a serving plate. Garnish with marron glacé or chocolate and serve with extra cream.

Serves 6

Iced Orange Pecan Mousse

Iced Orange Pecan Mousse

6 egg whites

140g (4¹/₂oz) caster sugar

600ml (1pt) double cream, whipped

1 tblspn finely chopped candied peel, optional

Praline

125g (4oz) sugar

60g (2oz) pecan halves

Custard Sauce

600ml (1pt) milk

rind of 1 orange

6 egg yolks

90g (3oz) sugar

Caramelised Peel

2 oranges

60g (2oz) sugar

1 To make praline, melt sugar with pecans in a small, heavy saucepan over low heat, stirring once or twice, then cook until sugar turns a rich caramel. Pour onto an oiled baking sheet and cool. Break into pieces, saving a few pecan halves for decoration. Crush remainder in a food processor and set aside.

2 Beat egg whites to soft peaks and gradually beat in caster sugar. Fold in whipped cream, crushed praline and candied peel, (if using). Pour mixture into two deep ring tins, cover with foil and refrigerate overnight.

3 To make sauce, scald milk with orange rind, then remove from heat. Beat egg yolks with sugar until pale and thick. Gradually stir in hot milk, then return mixture to saucepan. Cook over low heat, stirring, until custard coats the spoon. Strain and set aside.

4 To caramelise peel, remove rind from oranges, scrape off pith and cut peel into matchsticks. Place in a small saucepan, cover with cold water, bring to the boil, drain and refresh under cold water. Return peel to pan, add the 60g (2oz) sugar and enough water to moisten. Cook over moderate heat until sugar dissolves and liquid evaporates. Remove from heat and set aside to cool.

5 Turn mousses onto serving plates and decorate with reserved pecan pieces and caramelised peel.

Serves 12

Christmas Trifle

10 sponge fingers

250g (8oz) crisp Italian almond macaroons

250ml (8fl oz) sherry or a mixture of sherry and brandy

500g (1lb) strawberries, hulled and halved

250g (8oz) blueberries or raspberries

English Egg Custard

375ml (12fl oz) milk

vanilla bean or 1/2 tspn vanilla essence

3 egg yolks

3 tblspn caster sugar

1 1/2 tspn cornflour

Lemon Syllabub

2 tblspn lemon juice

brandy

thinly peeled rind of 1 lemon

75g (2 1/2 oz) caster sugar

315ml (10fl oz) double cream

90ml (3fl oz) white wine

1 To start syllabub, place lemon juice in a measuring cup, add enough brandy to measure 125ml (4fl oz), add lemon rind, cover and stand overnight.

2 To make custard, scald milk in a saucepan with vanilla bean (if using). Beat egg yolks, sugar and cornflour until light. Remove bean from milk and gradually stir into egg mixture. Return mixture to saucepan and cook over low heat, stirring, until custard coats the back of the spoon. Pour into a bowl, stir in vanilla essence (if using) cover surface with plastic food wrap and cool.

3 Halve sponge fingers and place in a shallow bowl with macaroons. Sprinkle with sherry and set aside to soak for 30 minutes. Reserve a few strawberries for garnish, then layer soaked biscuits, strawberries and blueberries or raspberries in a glass serving bowl. Spoon custard over, cover and chill.

4 To finish syllabub, strain lemon liquid, pressing rind well to extract flavour. Add sugar to liquid and stir until dissolved. Beat cream to soft peaks then gradually add lemon liquid and wine, a little at a time, beating constantly until cream holds soft peaks. Cover and chill.

5 An hour before serving, spoon syllabub over trifle. When ready to serve, decorate with reserved berries.

Serves 8-10

Christmas Trifle

Index

Managing Editor: Rachel Blackmore
Editors: Kirsten John, Linda Venturoni
Production Manager: Anna Maguire
Picture Editor: Kirsten Holmes
Production Editor: Sheridan Packer
Editorial and Production Assistant: Danielle Thiris
Layout and Finished Art: Stephen Joseph

Published by J.B. Fairfax Press Pty Limited
80-82 McLachlan Avenue
Rushcutters Bay, NSW 2011
A.C.N. 003 738 430

Formatted by J.B. Fairfax Press Pty Limited
Printed by Toppan Printing Co, Hong Kong
PRINTED IN HONG KONG

© Margaret Fulton and Suzanne Gibbs (recipes)
© Ray Jarrett (photography)
© J.B. Fairfax Press Pty Limited (this edition), 1995

JBFP 384 A/UK
Includes Index
ISBN 1 86343 116 0 (set)
ISBN 1 86343 217 5

Distribution and Sales Enquiries
Australia: J.B. Fairfax Press Pty Limited
Ph: (02) 361 6366 Fax (02) 360 6262
United Kingdom: J.B. Fairfax Press Limited
Ph: (01933) 402330 Fax: (01933) 402234